A Parent's Survival Guide for Your Teenage Driver

Thomas Hund

Copyright © Thomas Hund 2019

All rights reserved. No part of this publication may be reproduced, stored in a retrieval system, or transmitted in any form or by any means, mechanical, photocopying, recording or otherwise, without prior permission in writing of the author.

ISBN: 9781705942239 (paperback)

Introduction

Driving a motor vehicle is probably the most dangerous activity in which your child will participate.

While most states require formal driver education in school (or driving school) for teenagers, the majority require no more than six hours of behind-the-wheel training. Many states require a minimum of fifty hours of behind-the-wheel instruction by parent or guardian. Some states also require that at least ten of these hours be driven at night. So you, the parent, will probably be the biggest influence on preparing your child to become a safe driver.

In this book you will be introduced to the IPDE system which is an organized method for you and your teenage driver to learn how to become an experienced defensive driver. Not only did this system help me behind the wheel with my students, it also helped me become a much safer driver in my own vehicle.

In my twenty years of teaching driver education at Wesclin High School, I instructed about 1,500 students behind the wheel.

I hope by sharing some of these experiences I can help you help your child prepare for a lifetime of safe driving habits.

Thomas Hund

Table of Contents

No Escape Path?

I had a student named John who was born and raised on a farm. He probably had been driving a farm truck since he was tall enough to reach the pedals. I would bet that when he entered my driver education classroom the first day he was most likely thinking – What do I need this class for? I already know how to drive! As luck or fate would have it, here is what happened to John behind the wheel in the Wesclin Driver Education car.

We had just completed an interstate drive, which John performed very well. We were heading through New Baden on our way back to the high school when this took place.

We were driving on the main road in town with a 30 mph speed limit when about two blocks ahead a delivery truck pulled over to the right to parallel park. As we were approaching the parked truck, we also had several oncoming cars, so I told John to "cover the brake". This means the driver needs to take their right foot away from the gas pedal and place it above the brake pedal. By covering the brake, the driver can now brake more quickly if needed. This also helps to make sure the driver does not hit the gas pedal when he/she meant to hit the brake pedal. What do you think happened next??

Remember we may not have an escape path because of the parked truck and the oncoming traffic. A couple of seconds later the driver of the truck jumped down and then stumbled into our lane right in front of us! I did not have to tell John to hit the brake pedal because we were both stomping on our brake pedals. We were able to stop a comfortable distance from the truck driver, but you should have seen the look on the truck driver's face! When we got back to school about five minutes later, guess what John asked me?

"Mr. Hund, how did you know that was going to happen?" Of course, I did not know the driver was going to stumble out into our path, but I identified that we were about to enter an area with no "escape path" so I told John. "Remember we always want to predict the worst."

This situation was a great example of how the IPDE driving system can help avoid a collision. In this book, I hope I can convince you to learn and help teach your young driver this method to become an excellent defensive driver.

IPDE Process

An Excellent Method to Become a Defensive Driver

While I was taking classes for my driver education certification at Eastern Illinois University, I remember reading about the IPDE process as part of our homework. I was definitely a better student in my 30's and 40's than I was in my teens and early 20's. It wasn't until I had taught Driver Education a couple of years that I realized just how important this system was to our safety in the driver education car and in my own vehicle.

The author of our textbook Drive Right explains the system as follows: "The IPDE system is an organized way for seeing, thinking and responding during the driving task". IPDE is an acronym for: Identify, Predict, Decide and Execute.

Identify – identify important information in the current driving situation

Predict – predict when and where possible points of conflict may develop

Decide – decide when, where, and how to communicate, adjust speed, and/or change position to avoid a conflict

Execute – execute the correct action(s) to prevent conflict

After a few years we modified this system to best work for us. Following is how we tried to use the IPDE Process.

Identify – Identify anything that could possibly cause you a problem as you are driving. In short – identify all possible hazards. Of course, most of this information will be in front of you, but you must still be concerned with what is going on behind you and beside you.

Predict – After you have identified something that could cause a problem – PREDICT THE WORST – predict the other driver, bike rider, pedestrian etc... is going to pull out in front of you, turn in front of you, walk out in front of you etc.

Decide – Decide what you are going to do if your prediction comes true. Are you going to brake, accelerate, steer, honk, or a combination of these to avoid, or at least lessen, the severity of the collision?

Execute – Do it!!! Execute your plan by physically braking, steering, accelerating and/or honking.

I believe when using this system you may get 5-10 seconds to move from the identify step to the execute step. This may not seem like a lot of time but is much better than failing to identify the possible hazard or predict the worst and then being caught off guard and having to make a quick decision. This could easily lead to a poor decision, especially for a beginning driver.

Following is one of my favorite examples of how the IPDE system worked for us in the driver education car:

He Risked His Life for What?

We were approaching Trenton on a two-way highway with a speed limit of 55 mph when up ahead there was a bicycle rider on our side of the road going the same direction as we were traveling. There was no oncoming traffic and no traffic behind us, so I did not say anything to my driver until we got closer to the bike rider. At this point, I told our driver to "slow down, slow down, slow down". As we were preparing to minimize the hazard by giving this bike rider a lot of space as we prepared to pass, what do you think the bike rider did? (Remember you are supposed to predict the worst!) Without checking traffic behind him, the bicyclist cut across both lanes to the opposite shoulder, right in front of us! Believe it or not, the bicyclist risked his life for an aluminum can! Luckily I had seen this man many times along the highway collecting cans before this encounter so I knew what might happen.

Let's look at how the IPDE system worked for us that day.

Identify – A bike rider on the right side of the road heading the same direction as we were. It was also very important to notice that we had no oncoming traffic and no traffic close behind.

Predict – The bike rider could cut in front of our path of travel or could possibly fall.

Decide – To slow to a safe speed so that if our prediction came true, we would be able to stop or steer gently to avoid a collision.

Execute – All we had to do in this situation was brake to avoid the bike rider who cut in front of us.

Keep in mind, I had to tell my driver to "slow down, slow down, slow down". Which of the four steps do you think my driver failed to accomplish? My driver saw the bike rider but either failed to identify the bike as a potential hazard or did not "Predict the Worst". Just seeing objects ahead or behind is not enough, you must identify these as potential hazards.

Following is a newspaper article from October 1965 that involved me:

"Tom Hund Struck by Car; Not Seriously Injured"

Tom Hund, four-year-old son of Mr. and Mrs. Jim Hund, suffered cuts and abrasions when he was struck by a car in the west end of town at 4:45 p.m. Tuesday.

Tom darted across the street from the north to the south side near the Proffitt store and was hit by a car. He was taken to Dr. Larson in a Moll ambulance and examined and later was taken to the hospital for x-rays which showed no broken bones. His head was bruised considerably but he apparently suffered no serious injury.

Following is your homework assignment:

If you had been the driver of this car,

#1 – How could you have used the IPDE System to avoid hitting "Little Mr. Hund"

#2 – Come up with a common example of how a driver can avoid or lessen the impact of a collision by using the IPDE system. (Try to come up with a realistic situation.)

#3 – How can this system help you on a daily basis?

Identify – The driver should have identified me or my brother and his friends along the side of the road. Seeing a four-year-old could certainly be very difficult but I was still on the south side of Main Street (35 mph speed limit) as my middle brother and several of his friends had already crossed to the north side.

Predict – The driver should predict that any of these young pedestrians could cross his path of travel.

Decide – The driver should slow firmly and be prepared to stop or possibly steer to avoid the children.

Execute – The driver should brake and or steer correctly to avoid the children.

In this situation what do you think the driver failed to do that ultimately led to me getting hit by the car? As a driver education teacher, I believe the driver most likely failed to identify the children on either side of the road. I also believe if the driver would have seen children ahead he definitely would have slowed down early as he approached Little Mr. Hund.

Regarding #2 of the homework assignment, I hope you came up with a great example. Here are the two most common times I had to instruct my drivers to "cover the brake".

- We are approaching a 4-way intersection: the vehicles from the left and right have a stop or yield sign so we have right of way, and a vehicle is approaching from our left or right. Why shouldn't we just continue on through the intersection with our right foot on the gas pedal? Once again, if your foot is still on the gas you either did not identify the vehicle approaching from the side as a potential hazard or did not predict the worst. Where is the most dangerous place on a 2-way road? Without a doubt, the most dangerous place is an intersection. This is a great example of an excellent driver preparing to avoid a collision that would be the other driver's fault. Following is how I would use the IPDE system for this situation:

Identify – The driver should first identify there's an intersection ahead (the most dangerous place) and a vehicle is approaching from the left or right.

Predict – The driver should predict the approaching vehicle could pull out into their path of travel.

Decide – As soon as the driver identifies the approaching car he/she should cover the brake and if necessary slow gently to prepare for what might happen. Can the driver stop to avoid the collision or is there a safe place to steer?

Execute – Physically brake and/or steer to avoid or at the very least lessen the impact.

- We are approaching a 4-way intersection with an oncoming car with the left turn signal on. Once again, I want my student to cover the brake and predict that the oncoming car might turn in front of them. In this situation it is totally dependent upon how far away the oncoming car is from the intersection and our speed.

Here is your "pop quiz" on the IPDE system. (This is the actual quiz I gave my students the following day in class. Let's see how you do!)

#1 – When using the IPDE system what is it you are trying to identify?

#2 – When using the IPDE system after you have made an identification, what should you predict?

#3 – After making your prediction, what should you be deciding to do about it?

#4 – When you reach the Execute stage, what does this mean you are doing?

#5 – Which of the four steps of the IPDE system do you think is the most important and why? You are only allowed to give one answer. You are not allowed to say they are all important, you must pick just one. No answer will be marked wrong as long as you do a good job of explaining why you chose your answer.

First before giving you my answer to #5, what do you think was usually the most common answer given by my classroom students?

The most popular answer by my students was the Execute step and their most common reason was that it doesn't matter how you handle the first three steps, you still must physically control the car. But I disagree!

After using the IPDE system now for about 25 years, I am convinced that the most important step is Identify. I believe that unless you identify something around you as a possible hazard, you will not make any kind of prediction and just as importantly you will not be planning any kind of decision to help you avoid a collision. Therefore, by failing to identify a potential hazard and not predicting or deciding, you could easily get into a situation that there is no "way out" except trying to lessen the impact of a collision-as with the delivery truck example described earlier.

Now a couple more questions.

#1 – When using the IPDE process, should the steps be done in order (I-P-D-E)?

True – Fortunately most of your predictions will be wrong so you will not get all the way to the execute stage. So you need to start over and try to identify the next potential hazard.

#2 – When using the IPDE system, should all of your predictions come true?

False

Can you imagine what driving would be like if all of your predictions (predict the worst) came true? As an experienced driver we understand that most of the time vehicles, bicycles, or pedestrians won't pull out or walk out in front of you, but if you are going to be an excellent defensive driver you have to be ready every time.

Throughout this book I hope I can convince you that

not only should the IPDE system be used by your young driver, but you also should use it when driving. I did not take college driver education courses until I was 33 years old and since using the IPDE system the only collisions I have had are striking a deer and a dog. Both of these collisions occurred on rural highways at night. I always tried to teach my students that when faced with these types of situations, the most important action is to stay in control of the vehicle. The vehicle can be repaired. I think one of the most common mistakes drivers make when they encounter an animal on a rural road at night is to attempt an emergency swerve. At highway speed this swerve must be done precisely. If you oversteer you could easily lose control which could cause severe injury or death.

Now for the rest of the story about Little Mr. Hund getting hit by the car in October of 1965...

I was tagging along with my middle brother Crickett and several of his friends. I am sure I thought tagging along was great, but I am positive my brother and his friends were not very excited to have me around. We were walking around town collecting bottle caps from the local gas stations. Everything was going fine until we needed to cross Main Street. My brother and his friends successfully crossed the street but I remained on the other side. Supposedly one of my brother's friends yelled "Come on Tom, you can make it!" The author of the newspaper article said that I had "darted" across the street. I don't think the author knew how slow I really was. Of course, I did not make it and was struck somewhere around the middle of the street and then flew in the air 25-30 feet until I landed on the sidewalk on the other side of Main Street. The article also said I had cuts and abrasions on my head and I was most likely unconscious.

What do you think my brother did? He did what most 6-year-olds probably would have done in this situation – He ran home! We lived only a few blocks away from the accident scene. Now according to my mother, here is what happened next. Crickett ran through the front door and yelled "Mom, Mom – Tom is lying on the middle of Main Street with a hole in his head!" Can you imagine what my mother was thinking? At this point my oldest brother Mike, grabbed Crickett and was yelling that he had killed their little brother. I'm sure mom broke the record for the ½ mile run and found me on the sidewalk not the middle of Main Street. I certainly don't remember much about the collision, but I do remember some things at the hospital. I remember eating a lot of Jello and getting a set of dominoes. According to my Uncle Gene, when he came to visit he asked me how I felt. I told him "Uncle Gene, I felt just like a jet plane". That is, I felt like a jet plane until I crash landed on the sidewalk.

This event certainly reminds me how lucky I am to be alive today, and also how amazing it is not to have been more seriously injured. But as a driver education teacher, I've thought a lot about how the driver must have felt when he hit me. I also have thought about how he would have felt if I had been killed or seriously injured.

So, whenever you are driving with your young drivers and you identify walkers, joggers, runners or bike riders please remember to "Predict the Worst"!

One last question about the IPDE system. When using the system how many of the steps are physical skills and how many are mental?

Identify – Mental
Predict – Mental
Decide – Mental
Execute – Physical

Not only are 3 of the 4 steps mental, but they are also the first 3 steps of the process, which have to be done in order to be effective. I believe becoming an excellent driver is more mental than physical. I also believe physical skills are very important, but after using this system for about 25 years in the driver education car and my own vehicle, I am certain that if you aren't paying very close attention at all times, you could easily get yourself into a situation in which there is no way to avoid a collision.

Pretest - First Day of Class

Here is a sample of a pretest I gave the students the first day of class. After the test, I let the students grade their own work, but by asking the class for answers as we graded it, I know it was rare to have anyone pass the test. My main goal was to try to show the class that each of them, no matter how much experience they have, will have a lot to learn. After the test, I asked the class if they thought these were all legitimate questions. Usually everyone agreed that they were.

Let's see how you would have done. (Answers follow the quiz.)

1. This question has 2 parts. A) Will the vehicle(s) you drive at home have ABS? I would then ask if anyone knew what ABS stood for. Usually a few might know that it stands for Anti-Lock-Brake System. I told them this was the only question they could get correct simply by answering it. The

possible answers were: yes, no, or I don't know. B) What is the main difference of driving a vehicle with or without ABS?

2. Where is the most dangerous place on a 2-way highway? Hint: this is the place that has the most collisions and fatalities. I also told them I just needed a one word answer.
3. True or False – You are approaching a flashing red light, which means you are approaching a four-way stop.
4. You are traveling at 55 mph on a dry, level and paved highway with your foot on the gas pedal and suddenly you need to make an emergency stop on the highway. In distance traveled, how many feet will it take you to stop your vehicle?
5. What is the minimum safe following distance (the least amount of distance you should leave between your car and the vehicle in front of you)? To get this answer correct you have to give me a number and a word.
6. What is the most common type of collision between a car and a motorcycle? Hint: It is definitely the fault of the driver of the car. For example I told the class if they guess a rear end collision that would be a type of collision but not the correct answer. That is all of the hints I can give you.

7. What is the only traffic sign you will always find on the left side of the highway? This sign is usually found in rural areas.
8. A two part question about hydroplaning: First we defined what this term means to the driver of a vehicle. We usually defined it as driving over a "puddle-collection" of water and suddenly your car has left the surface of the road and you now have NO TRACTION. A) If your car starts to hydroplane, how will you know? B) Now that you know you are hydroplaning what action(s) should you take?
9. When is it legal to drive past a school bus when it is loading or unloading students? Tell me what type of road you are on and where is the bus located as compared to your vehicle.
10. You are approaching an intersection and planning on going straight ahead. Explain to me how you are going to check for cross traffic to make sure it is safe before entering the intersection.

Answers:

1. A) Most students answered "I don't know" but usually only a few really knew what ABS was all about. Remember you got the answer to part A correct as long as you gave an honest answer. B) Anti-Lock Brakes are

designed to allow the driver to press very firmly on the brake pedal and still be able to steer. A short film we watched said ABS allows the system to pump the brakes 18 times per second, so you should not go into a skid and lose control. The film also reminded us that when you brake firmly and the ABS takes over you may hear a bumping sound and may feel some vibration from the brake pedal but this is normal. I am not sure ABS will help you on ice or loose gravel, but it is supposed to help the driver stay in control on dry or wet pavement.

2. The most dangerous place on a two-way highway is by far the intersections. Our textbook states that nearly one-half of all crashes and nearly one-fourth of fatalities occur at intersections. I did not want my students to be scared when approaching an intersection but I wanted them to approach every intersection with caution.
3. The answer is False. Believe it or not, in most of my classes, no one got this answer correct. As we graded this question I asked, "Whoever thinks the answer is true, raise your hand." Usually, every hand went up! The main reason I asked this question was because the two biggest towns in our school district each has an intersection with a

flashing red light and each of the intersections are 4-way stops. We do not have any red, yellow, and green traffic lights in either town. I told them that if they see a flashing red light as they are approaching an intersection, this only guarantees that **they** need to stop. It does not mean cars approaching from their left or right have a stop sign or red light. A few times in my driving career I have been at a stop sign and the sign below the stop sign said, "ONCOMING TRAFFIC DOES NOT STOP". I think **these** are very dangerous. I also told them during their driving time with me I would take them to several intersections with a flashing red light that might be a two way or only a one way stop. I also reminded them sometimes when they reach a two-way stop it might have a sign below that says "Cross Traffic Does Not Stop". Finally, I told them every time they approach a stop sign, it is their job to determine who does and who does not have to stop!

4. I told the students they certainly did not have to get this answer exactly right as long as they were close. I doubt many drivers that are out on the roads today would come close to the answer. Let's break this into parts. Remember your foot was on the

gas when you had to slam on the brake. It sounds like you must not have identified the hazard early, predicted the worst or maybe you were following too closely. It takes the average driver (and remember we want to be excellent) about ¾ of a second to move their foot from the gas pedal to the brake pedal and at 55 mph you are traveling at 81 feet per second. Please don't try this when you are driving but as a passenger your perspective sure changes when you look out the front windshield at highway speed (it doesn't look that fast) but when you look at the pavement or ground out your side window, 81 feet per second sure is fast! Therefore, ¾ of a second is roughly 60 feet. So your car has traveled about 4 car lengths before you even got to the brake pedal. Our text also stated that the braking distance at this speed is about 150 feet so your actual stopping distance is about 210 feet. Believe it or not the two most common answers from my students was 10 or 15 feet. Even at 25 mph it takes the average driver 56 feet to make a complete stop. As they say, "You can't stop on a dime!"

5. The minimum safe following distance recommended by our textbook is 3 seconds. I would recommend 4 seconds or more for your beginning driver to be safe. Keep in

mind that your inexperienced driver will probably have a much more difficult time recognizing potential hazards then you and I might. My rule in the driver education car was whenever I identified a hazard that I thought my driver failed to see I would tell them to cover the brake. When it comes to safe driving, it is impossible to replace experience! Using seconds for following distance works very well since this means the faster you are driving the more distance you will leave between you and the vehicle in front. Whenever someone is following you too closely, I would suggest, even if you have to slow down a little, to be sure to give the vehicle ahead even more space. When you are being followed too closely, the last thing you want your driver to do is slam on the brake and risk a rear end collision. As you probably know, it is the car that gets rear ended that usually gets the worst of the impact.

6. The most common collision between a car and a motorcycle is a side impact collision in which the driver of the car turns left in front of an oncoming motorcyclist. We had many students turn in articles for a homework assignment about this exact collision. In fact, shortly after the Pittsburgh Steelers won the Super Bowl in 2006, Ben Roethlisberger

was severely injured when a driver made a left turn in front of his motorcycle. I would bet most drivers who have been at fault for this type of collision would probably tell the police, "I didn't see the motorcycle!"

7. The only sign you will always find on the left side of the road is (if you need another hint it is the shape of a pennant or if you are good at math it is the shape of an isosceles triangle) the no passing zone sign. When I had my learner's permit this sign was not posted. All we had were white and black "Do Not Pass" signs on the right side of the highway. This new yellow pennant shape is much more effective since we have to check to our left to see if traffic is clear to pass.
8. A) The best way to describe how you will know you are hydroplaning is you will "feel it". B) If your vehicle begins to hydroplane the only thing you should do is take your foot off the gas pedal and wait until you feel you have regained traction.
9. The only time it is legal to drive past a school bus when it is loading or unloading students is when you are on a four-lane road and the bus is on the opposite side of the road. No matter what lane you are in on a one-way or two-way road you must legally stop for a school bus.

10. As you are approaching an intersection, make sure your driver at a minimum checks for cross traffic by checking left, right, left and right again. Do not allow your driver to just check left then right and enter an intersection. I can't tell you how many times in my car or the driver education car I or a student would check left (clear), check right (clear), check left again (NOT CLEAR). Wow! Where was that vehicle the first time I checked? A good way to practice this skill is to drive straight ahead on side streets for as many blocks as you can. Work with your driver on checking both directions and double checking both directions before entering every intersection. If your view to the left is blocked by houses, trees, buildings etc., you may want to check to the right first, then left, right, left.

Scariest Experience (by a longshot!)

We were traveling west on a highway with a 55 mph speed limit with a student driver who had about ten hours of total driving experience (school and home combined). There were three or four oncoming cars heading east at highway speed. Without any warning one of the oncoming cars pulled out to pass as if our driver education car was invisible! We were about one to two seconds away from a head on collision at highway speed! What do you think my driver did.............?

My driver just FROZE! She did not hit the brake or try to steer to avoid the collision. Luckily, I had faced some potential head on collisions in my driving career so I didn't have to stop and think – I just reacted. I firmly hit the instructor's brake and was able to grab the top of the steering wheel and steer our car to the paved shoulder on our right. As we pulled to the shoulder, the passing car went right past us in our westbound lane! As I brought the car to a stop on the shoulder, the poor driver was sobbing. I wasn't sobbing but I sure was sweating! I certainly don't blame the driver for freezing that day because I am sure she had never experienced anything like that before. I reassured her that this was not her fault and we were all okay. Of course, she was done driving for the day. When we got back to school, I told our principal what happened and kiddingly asked if I could have the rest of the day off. When this student drove with me again, we drove a couple of times in town so she would not have to worry about highway speed until she was ready.

This incident reinforced the idea that EVERY oncoming car is a potential hazard. This also was a great example of whenever you are driving, but especially at highway speed, you must know if you have an escape path on your right and be prepared to use it!

A couple of years later I was discussing this situation in class and one of my students asked what the observer (student in the backseat) said about this incident. I told this student, "You know Bob, why don't you ask him?" The next day I asked her if she had talked with Bob and she said that she had so I asked her what he said. She said, "He thought he was going to poop in his pants – but he didn't say poop." I couldn't have said it better myself.

How do you think the IPDE system worked for me in this situation?

I – Identify three or four oncoming cars as potential hazards

P – Predict that one of the cars might cross the center line

D – Decide what to do if car crosses center line **(brake and steer right onto paved shoulder)**

E – Execute by braking and steering to shoulder on the right

Minimize a Hazard, Separate Hazards and Compromise Space

The author of Drive Right used three terms to help drivers deal with a hazard or hazards on the roadways. The first, "Minimize a Hazard", should not be too difficult as long as you identify the hazard early enough. The second, "Separate Hazards", is more difficult because you have to deal with multiple hazards. If these hazards are identified early, this also shouldn't be too difficult. But if you must "Compromise Space", this could be a "hair-raising" experience.

Minimize a Hazard – This should be the easiest of the three since you only have to deal with one hazard. The author's definition is to "put more distance between yourself and the hazard". For example, you may be driving and identify a parked car along your side of the road ahead but you do not have any oncoming traffic. Be sure traffic is clear behind you and have your driver steer gently and allow plenty of space from the parked car. You may want to remind your driver this parked car (potential hazard) could also pull out (with or without a turn signal) or one of the doors could open, so be sure to give them plenty of space. This could be more difficult if the hazard ahead is a pedestrian or bicyclist. Keep in mind a pedestrian or bicyclist could do anything as you approach. Be sure to have your driver slow down even more for a pedestrian or bicyclist.

Separate Hazards – This needs to occur when you face more than one hazard. The author's definition is "decide to adjust your speed to let them separate so you can deal with only one hazard at a time".

First Example – You are approaching a parked car on the right side of a street but you also have an oncoming car. You will most likely need to adjust your speed so you don't meet the oncoming car in the same area as the parked car. If your driver is not sure of what to do, I would suggest they slow down and let the oncoming car go first. Since the parked car is on your side of the street, you should be the one to yield to the oncoming car. If the hazard on your side of the street is a pedestrian or bike rider, I would suggest slowing down even more to be sure not to meet the multiple hazards at the same time.

Second example – We faced this problem many

times when we drove on backroads which we defined as a narrow rural road with no lane markings and usually no speed limit signs. In the distance we identified a narrow concrete bridge and an oncoming car. Of course, the last thing we wanted to do was meet the oncoming car on or anywhere near the bridge. If we had any doubt of who was going to reach the bridge first, I would instruct my student to slow down and let the other driver cross the bridge first. We also made sure to move to the right to give the oncoming car plenty of space.

I don't think separating hazards should be too difficult as long as you identify multiple hazards as early as possible so you have extra time and space to make a good decision.

But now for the scary one!

Compromise Space – According to our author, "Sometimes hazards cannot be minimized or separated. When this occurs, you must decide to compromise space by giving as much space as possible to the greater hazard." This definition might sound easy enough, but let me give you an example of this type of situation.

In the Blink of an Eye

I was driving an 8-passenger school van back to school after a golf match. We were on a 2-way highway with a speed limit of 55 mph about two miles from the high school. It was night-time and I identified an oncoming well-lit semi-truck. I certainly identified this semi as a potential hazard and thankfully I did, because I can still visualize what happened next. As I was preparing to meet this oncoming truck which was being driven safely in the correct lane, I suddenly identified two oncoming bicyclists without headlights in my lane just inside the white line on my right! I quickly realized that I did not have the time or space to separate these hazards. I read somewhere that when driving at night with your low beam headlights on you can only identify objects without reflective material about 100 feet ahead. At 55 mph you are traveling at 81 feet per second, so I only had between one and two seconds to complete the IPDE system. I believe this is the scariest one or two seconds of my driving career! I steered a few inches to my left but there was no way I could risk the lives of the 6 students in the van by risking a possible head on collision with the semi-truck. Fortunately, I was able to somehow avoid colliding with the semi and either of the bicyclists. Immediately after I avoided this potential catastrophe, I asked the golfers in the back of the van if they saw what happened. I was told that some were sleeping and some were talking and not paying attention. If I would have collided with one or both bicyclists, there would have been no eyewitnesses in the van. If I had not had the students along with me, I think I would have tried to turn around and see if I could find out the identities of the two bicyclists.

Do you think we discussed this event in my driver education classes the next day? You bet we did! So much for lesson plans! After discussing the terms "Minimize a Hazard" and "Separate Hazards", I explained to the students why compromising space can be so difficult. I explained how scary this situation was for me the night before and how close I came to colliding with one or both bicyclists. It certainly would have been safer if the bicyclists had lights on the front of their bikes. If they would have been riding the same direction I was traveling, I may have been able to see the bikes' reflectors sooner. I told the students that without a doubt this was the scariest experience I had ever faced behind the wheel.

I also asked the students this question: If I would have been facing this exact same situation during daylight hours would this have made any difference in how I would have handled it? I am sure some of my less experienced students thought this was a trick question. Of course you and I know during daylight hours this would have been easy to "separate the hazards" because I would have been able to identify the bicyclists much sooner. I hope this story reminds you how important it is to have your student driver get as much night time driving experience as possible. Many inexperienced drivers don't know how much more difficult and dangerous it is to drive at night.

Now for the most unbelievable part of the story!

After we finished the lesson in my last class of the day, the students left the classroom except one. This student told me he was one of the bicyclists from the night before. He also told me I almost got them killed last night. I took a deep breath and responded by telling him – "No, you two almost got yourselves killed last night." I said, "You two should have seen my headlights for a long time as I was approaching." Then I asked, "Why didn't you two go off the road?" He said they thought I would "move over for them." I told him if I hadn't had an oncoming semi, I would have moved over to the other lane. He did admit they were not aware of the oncoming semi since it was coming up from behind them.

I think the most common error for an inexperienced driver in this situation is after identifying that the bicyclists were so close, he/she may have jerked the steering wheel to the left and may have collided with the oncoming semi.

I hope you or your young driver never has to face a situation like this. But after having this situation happen to me, I am convinced driving, especially at night, is for most of us, the most dangerous thing we will do in our lifetimes.

Point of No Return

Thankfully the Driver Ed Teacher was in the Backseat!

A couple of years ago my two older brothers and I were on our way to Lambert Airport in St. Louis. With just the three of us in the car, guess where I was sitting? No, I was not driving. Do you think my older brothers were going to let me drive? I also was not sitting in the front passenger's seat. I don't think my older brother wanted a driver education teacher critiquing his driving. So, I tried my best not to be a backseat driver. As Crickett was driving toward a green traffic light, it turned yellow. My oldest brother Mike (definitely the most conservative of the brothers) was yelling go, go, go and at the same time Crickett is brake, brake, braking and I was in the back seat laugh, laugh laughing! As we waited for the red light to turn green, Crickett and Mike were having a discussion about who was right or wrong. I was definitely not going to be the deciding vote. This was not a dangerous situation because there was no other vehicle approaching the intersection.

I still chuckle whenever I think about this story, but this is not what you want to have happen when your son/daughter is driving toward a traffic light. As he/she is approaching a green traffic light that suddenly turns yellow, you do not want to be yelling go, go, go while your driver is braking or yelling stop, stop, stop while your driver is accelerating. At best this would be a very tense situation and at worst could lead to a collision.

When my students were approaching a green traffic light, we were always trying to determine the location of our "Point of No Return." The author of our textbook defined the point of no return as the point at which you could no longer stop without entering the intersection. He also defined the point of no return as roughly two seconds before the intersection. As we were approaching a green light, I always asked my driver to tell me when he/she reached the point of no return. At first, most of my drivers would think the point of no return was much farther from the intersection then it really was. The nearest traffic light to Wesclin High School was about 10 miles away so we were not able to get a lot of practice with the point of no return. This is a good example of how parents are going to need to be the teacher for the point of no return. This will take a lot of practice since drivers will be approaching green traffic lights at many different speeds.

When we were practicing with traffic lights, I would ask my drivers how many times they had gone straight through an intersection when the light was yellow. A few of my students said one or two but the vast majority said none. I think this is another very important skill that each student must master before becoming a licensed driver. Try to help your son/daughter by taking them to many green traffic lights and just as importantly, at different speeds.

But...Can You Apply It?

My favorite green traffic light experience happened early in my career. I had a student approaching a circular green traffic light on a four-lane highway with a 55 mph speed limit. My driver was approaching the intersection about 50 mph with her foot over the brake. We did not have any traffic approaching the intersection from our front, back or sides so I asked her to tell me when she thought she had reached the point of no return. Keep in mind that most students picked the point of no return too soon. About 4 or 5 seconds later she said "Now!" Surprisingly, this was the exact moment that I was selecting our point of no return. About one second later, the light changed to yellow and guess what my driver did? She hit the brake pedal firmly, which was a surprise to me since I felt she did a good job of selecting our point of no return. I then said "Let off the brake, let off the brake, let off the brake." When giving important commands, I tried not to yell but used a firm tone to let the student know how important it was to follow the command. I felt if our student brought the car to a stop, we would have been in the intersection.

Luckily, we did not have any traffic behind us that day because this unexpected braking could have caused a rear end collision. This potential collision would not have been our fault (the driver behind should legally be able to stop without striking the car in front), but if there is a rear end collision it is normally the car in front that takes the "worst of the wallop!"

After this event I made sure to really emphasize to the students how important not only knowing the definition of Point of No Return is, but even more importantly, knowing how to apply it.

Are You Going or Waiting?

One of the most important things I learned on the job behind the wheel was I could not read the driver's mind, so I came up with a phrase that really worked well at intersections. Whenever I had a student preparing to make a left turn and we had oncoming traffic, meaning the oncoming traffic had the right of way, I would firmly ask my driver "Are you going or waiting?" and sometimes I repeated the phrase. I needed to know as soon as possible what my driver was thinking about the speed and distance of this oncoming vehicle.

If the student said, "I am going" and the oncoming vehicle was a safe distance away, I let the driver go ahead and make the turn.

But if the driver said, "I am going" and the oncoming vehicle was too close, I would firmly say "No, we are waiting, slow down, slow down, slow down" and I was also prepared to grab the top of the steering wheel just in case.

If the driver said "Ummm", I told them that we are

going to wait since the driver was unsure. Our rule was – If you don't know, DON'T GO!

I also had a few times when students said "I am waiting" when the oncoming traffic was very far away. Sometimes I would tell the driver, "You have plenty of time go ahead and make the turn." Sometimes, especially if we had no one behind us, I would let the student wait and after the turn or sometimes even before the turn my driver would say, "I should have gone" even before I could ask them.

Being able to quickly judge the oncoming vehicle's speed and distance is not a skill many drivers know immediately. Some students were much better than others. Try to be patient with your driver and keep practicing this skill. No matter how skilled I felt my driver was, I always asked them "Are you going or waiting?" when preparing for a left turn with oncoming traffic nearby.

Another situation in which I would ask my driver "going or waiting" was when we were pulling out from a two-way stop, two-way yield, one way stop or one way yield with traffic coming from our left or right. The last thing we want in this situation is for our driver to dangerously pull out in front of traffic that has the right of way. This is another situation where you don't want to wait until it is too late to help your driver make a good decision. After gaining some valuable experience at this procedure, I felt there was a third step to this process, considering more than just speed and distance. I also felt I had to know the skill level of each of my drivers to make their left and right turns. I quickly learned that some drivers are much better than others at being able to accelerate through their turns when pulling out from a stop or yield sign into cross traffic. So this really became a three-step process.

1. What is the other vehicle's distance from the intersection?
2. What is the other vehicle's speed?
3. What is the ability of your driver to make this left or right turn?

Keep in mind your driver will need to learn how to handle these decisions at town and highway speeds. I think it would be great if you could have your driver handle these intersections starting with light traffic but as he/she progresses you will want them in situations with more traffic and also have them turn onto rural highways with much higher speeds.

Just Another Left Turn?

I can still vividly remember a "great" left turn with my daughter, Brittney, when she had her learner's permit. We were leaving the grocery store in New Baden during "rush hour" and as we walked to our car in the parking lot I warned her that this could be a very difficult left turn to enter the highway. I believe Brittney's response was "Oh sure, Dad." Believe it or not, we waited about two or three minutes – which I am sure felt like 2 or 3 hours to Brittney- before she was able to complete this left turn. As we were waiting I kept asking her to tell me when she thought she saw a safe gap for us to turn. The whole time we were waiting I only saw one small gap that I would have taken if I had been driving but Brittney did not think this gap was big enough. If you have a true beginner in this situation, you may want them to make a right turn in this situation, then later make a left turn so you can get turned around.

Remember you can't read your driver's mind so please ask them ahead of time, "Are you going or waiting? Are you going or waiting?" This really worked well for me.

Another teaching skill I learned from my instructor at Eastern Illinois University was to be sure not to randomly tell your driver to "make a left turn here" (especially don't tell your driver too late!). I would be sure to tell the student "at the next intersection make a left or right turn," so he/she would have plenty of time to signal and slow down before the turn. I also might say "Do you see the IGA sign way up ahead on your left?" If they said yes, I would them instruct them to turn into the IGA parking lot. This was an excellent way to check "when" the driver would use their turn signal since the parking lot was several blocks ahead. I wanted to be sure the student didn't use the turn signal too soon because you don't want your turn signal on as you pass by other streets or parking lots before you actually make the turn. I wanted to be sure my students used their turn signals for every turn, but more importantly, at the proper time.

As my drivers progressed I also asked them to be able to read street signs (usually green) to find the correct place to turn. Of course it was much easier to find 1st Street, 2nd Street, 3rd Street etc.. But I also had them try to find Oak Street, Elm Street, Washington, Lincoln etc.. I did not want my students to be totally reliant on GPS systems. We also needed to be aware of the traffic behind us as we prepared for each turn. If we had someone "tailgating" us we would slow early and gently and signal as early as we could. The last thing we wanted to do with a tailgater is to brake suddenly and give a late turn signal. I also informed my students if he/she felt they were approaching a turn too fast, it would be okay to turn off your signal and turn at the next side road.

The ________________ is a Safety Device

During the first few weeks of my driver education career I had a student who was stopped in a safe position at a two-way stop on a quiet side road in Trenton. We had a pickup truck approaching from our right with a left turn signal flashing. This vehicle was definitely too close for us to pull out so we were just waiting for him to make his left turn. Unexpectedly the driver started turning way too soon and was coming right at us. What do you think my driver did? Not surprisingly, my driver did nothing. What do you think I did? If you were in my seat, what would you have done? As the driver of the truck was turning, I could see his head was turned away from his path of travel and directed toward a person who was walking in a parking lot across the road. Since the driver of the truck was "not watching where he was going" we had to get his attention ASAP. Without thinking, I reached across the vehicle and hit the horn with the palm of my left hand (center of the steering wheel). After hearing the horn, the driver turned his attention to us and was able to swerve around us to avoid a collision, but it was close. This was a perfect example of how to teach my students that the HORN is a Safety Device!

Before you take the first drive with your son/ daughter, I would suggest you let them honk the horn a few times. Keep in mind the horn is not always in the center of the steering wheel. I owned a little Chevy Aveo recently that had "thumb horns". Although this was unusual to me, it did allow me to honk the horn without having to take either hand off the steering wheel. I also think it would be a good idea to have your driver practice different types of "honks". Whenever I approach bike riders or pedestrians (especially children) from behind I like to give them a couple of "friendly- gentle honks" to let them know I am approaching.

After that event I always shared this story with my classes. After I told the part where the pickup truck was coming right at us, I would quickly ask the entire class, "What would you do – right now?" Most students did not answer, but a few would say "honk the horn" or "back up". Backing up would not be a bad answer as long as the driver would remember to shift to reverse and also make sure no one was behind them. All I know is it would not be the fault of the driver behind you if you were to back into them trying to avoid the collision.

A few final notes about this near collision with the pickup truck:

1. When I blared the horn as the truck was coming toward us, you should have seen the other driver's expression after he heard the horn. It was priceless!
2. After the driver was able to swerve around us, do you think he stopped to thank us for helping him avoid the collision? He did not, but I am sure he was glad there wasn't a story of this crash in the next week's local newspaper.
3. Do you think this potential head on collision was just as dangerous as the "poop my pants" situation? Of course not, because the pickup truck was probably going about 10 mph and we were standing still, but it was still very startling.

I tried to teach my students whenever they think some other roadway user does not see them approaching, they should use the horn to get the other driver's attention. Don't wait until it is too late to use the horn as a safety/warning device.

Safely and Legally Stopping at Stop Signs or Red Lights

Following are your quiz questions about this topic:

1. When stopping at a red light or stop sign, how should your driver know he/she has made a complete stop? When asking this question in the classroom, I once had a student say "the speedometer will say zero". When you are at a busy intersection, you don't want to be looking at the speedometer. I think the best answer is you know you have made a complete stop when you feel the car gently rock back.
2. When approaching a stop sign or red light what are the four things or places you must look for to make a safe and legal stop? For bonus points see if you can put them in the correct order.

One – you should look for a stop line (should be white).

Two – If there is no stop line, you should look for a crosswalk (two white parallel lines). Could there be an intersection that has both a marked stop line and crosswalk? Yes, you will usually find these at busy intersections especially with traffic lights.

Three – (this is a tricky one!) If there is no marked stop line or crosswalk, could there still be a crosswalk that you must legally stop behind? Once again, the answer is yes. If you approach an intersection with a sidewalk on each side of the intersection (no white markings!), this is still considered a crosswalk and you must legally and safely stop behind this "invisible" crosswalk. This situation is most commonly found on side streets in town. If you would strike a pedestrian in this "invisible" crosswalk, you would be at fault.

Four – If you approach a stop sign (not usually at a traffic light now) and there is no stop line, no marked crosswalk, or no sidewalks, where should you safely stop? Make sure you stop a "safe distance" from the intersection. I don't think there is an exact answer for this situation but you want to be sure you don't startle anyone who is approaching the intersection from your left or right on the crossroad ahead of you.

The Importance of Stopping at the Right Spot

I once had a student driving toward the main street of New Baden from a side street. As we approached there was no stop line and the crosswalk was almost completely faded. Since we were approaching the main road of town, do you think we had sidewalks on both sides of the intersection? You bet we did, so I made sure to instruct my student to be sure to stop safely behind the sidewalks. Just as we were about to stop in the safe and legal spot, a lady "popped out" from behind the tall building on our left. Who has right of way in this situation? Of course, the pedestrian does. As we made sure other traffic was clear, we gave a friendly wave to the pedestrian to allow her to use the very hard-to-see crosswalk. Now, what kind of expression do you think this lady gave my driver? No, you are wrong!! She gave us the biggest smile and waved, just because we stopped where we were supposed to stop.

Later I found an article in the local paper about undercover police who would approach crosswalks just as a vehicle was approaching a stop sign. If the driver did not stop in the safe and legal position and let the pedestrian safely cross they were given a "warning ticket". At the end of the article the undercover police stated "They Would Be Back" and this time they would be issuing "real" tickets!

On my students' final driving tests, they were graded on how they approached ten stop signs and each one was graded for not only making a "complete stop" but also for making sure the driver stopped at the safe and legal position.

Lane Changing (Seems like an easy maneuver but........)

I can still remember many of the important lessons I learned while attending driver education classes at Eastern Illinois University. One day my professor was taking a great deal of time discussing the difficulties and dangers of beginning drivers performing lane changes. I remember thinking lane changes should be easy since you only have to steer slightly to accomplish the maneuver. After observing some of my first students performing lane changes in the Wesclin driver education car, I soon realized this was not the case.

Following are some examples of the common errors I saw students make.

1. The student checked the blind spot over their LEFT shoulder when needing to perform a RIGHT lane change. No, I am not kidding!
2. Instead of glancing over their shoulder

toward their blind spot the student LOOKED over their shoulder (We defined a glance as something that should take less than a second) for too long and now the car was heading toward the center line or the edge of the road. Make sure you are prepared to help steer if your driver makes this type of mistake.

3. Instead of turning their head and neck, the student turned their body toward the blind spot. Now the car is heading for the other lane before the driver has checked to see if their blind spot is clear.
4. As the student checked their blind spot, their foot came off the gas pedal. My son Tyler had this problem when he first started driving, but he was quickly able to correct this with some extended practice.
5. Some students checked their mirrors but not their blind spots. This is another example of why you need to be one step ahead of your driver. You need to make a quick blind spot check before your driver does to be ready for this possible error.

The Best Thing About a Freshman Is When They Become a Sophomore

Once, I was driving the school van on the way back from a girls' golf match with three freshmen in the back of the van. We were on an interstate with 3 lanes of traffic going in both directions. I was in the center lane, catching up to a semi-truck and getting ready to pass on the left.

Now for a question. What do you think would be a step-by-step process for me to perform a lane change to prepare to pass this semi? Following is how I taught my students to lane change safely and legally.

1. Check your rearview and sideview mirrors (just in case someone is coming up fast!).
2. Check your blind spot. (Remember just a glance)
3. If both mirrors and blind spot are clear put on your turn signal.

4. Steer GENTLY to the other lane.
5. Don't forget to turn off your turn signal!

Now back to my situation in the van with the girls' golf team. First, I checked my mirrors and in my sideview mirror I saw two sports cars approaching very quickly. I would estimate their speed at 90-100 mph. (The times you feel like you are standing still when they pass you!) So, there was no need to perform step 2 (checking blind spot). I asked the girls to watch these passing cars and tell me how fast they thought they were traveling. Keep in mind they were all freshmen and would not be enrolled in driver education until their sophomore year.

The next thing I heard from the back of the van was some discussion. One of them asked, "How fast are you going?" Good question, no wonder all 3 of these girls were honor roll students. In fact, one of them went on to get her doctorate from Duke University. I glanced at my speedometer and told them 65 mph, which was the speed limit. More discussion! Finally, they came up with an answer. Guess what it was? Believe it or not they came up with 70mph. You and I know that if those cars had been going 70, it would have taken a long time for them to pass. This shows how little many students know about driving until they truly gain experience behind the wheel.

Luckily, my hometown of Mascoutah was only about 10 miles away and had a two-lane highway turn into a four-lane road as we entered town. The speed limit was only 30 mph, so I could observe the students performing lane changes at town speed, before attempting to pass on a two-way highway, or merging and lane changing on the interstate (expressway). Keep in mind any steering error by your driver will be hugely magnified when driving at highway or interstate speed. Oversteering at a high rate of speed could cause total loss of control!

Emergency Situations

In class before we discussed the different types of potential emergency situations one could face behind the wheel, we first defined the word "panic". Wikipedia defines it as a "sudden sensation of fear which is so strong as to dominate or prevent reason and logical thinking". Next I asked what they thought panic meant in terms of driving a vehicle. We usually all agreed on the following: When facing an emergency situation a driver usually panics when they "Do Not Know What To Do!" Following are some potential emergency situations your driver may face behind the wheel. Let's see if you know what to do.

Hydroplaning – According to Driversed.com this means you "have lost traction and are sliding on a film of water". If your vehicle begins to hydroplane, what are three things you should not do? You should not attempt to brake, accelerate or steer. Can you see what might happen to an inexperienced driver who panics in this situation? Any one of these three could cause the vehicle to go out of control. Most importantly, what should a driver do when faced with this emergency situation? I told my students that if your car starts to hydroplane, you should just take your foot off the gas pedal (and if you are religious, say a very quick prayer) and wait until you regain traction. Then I asked them this question – How are you going to know when your vehicle starts to hydroplane? Since I have experienced this several times in my driving career, I told them "You will be able to feel it and it is a scary feeling." Finally how are you going to know when your vehicle is no longer hydroplaning? Once again I told them, "You will feel it." Hopefully, after taking your foot off the gas pedal, it should only take a few seconds to regain traction control.

Off Road Recovery – This occurs when your front and possibly back rear tire(s) drop off the pavement onto dirt, mud, gravel, or grass. Because of this, the vehicle will most likely be shaking. Can you see how a beginning driver could panic now? How do you think a driver should SAFELY get this vehicle back on the road?

1. Remain calm because you know what to do!
2. Take your foot off the gas pedal and grab the steering wheel firmly because the vehicle will most likely be shaking.
3. Steer and counter steer gently to keep the vehicle under control.

4. Now you can GENTLY brake to a safe speed (textbook states 5-10 mph) and check traffic in front and behind. I believe an experienced driver can get back on the road at a higher speed than 5-10 mph but again I think it would be better for an inexperienced driver to perform a maneuver a little too slow instead of too fast!
5. If traffic is clear, especially in front of you, steer back onto the road.

This situation can be very dangerous for an inexperienced driver especially if they were distracted and did not notice their vehicle was headed off the road. The two most common errors drivers make are quickly jerking the wheel to the left or immediately slamming on the brake pedal.

If you oversteer left you could:

1. Wind up in the wrong lane which could cause a head on collision.
2. Lose control or even flip the vehicle because of the height of the pavement.

If you overbrake you could lose control of the vehicle since you only have two or three tires on pavement.

I think correctly handling an off road recovery is

something you can practice at home but I would recommend that you make sure you:

1. Have a safe area to the right of the road in case you go further off the road than you expected.
2. Be sure that traffic is clear all around you.
3. For the first few times, drive a speed much lower than 55 mph. Depending on your driver's skill level, I would recommend about 30 mph.

I believe off road recovery is going to be needed by all drivers at some point, so it is critical that your driver knows exactly what to do.

Tire Blowout – This happened when I was driving the boys' golf team to a match. I was driving west on the interstate in the right lane when suddenly **BOOM!** without any advanced warning my right front tire exploded! This was my first experience with a tire blowout. Luckily, I had been a driver education teacher for several years, so I not only knew what to do, I also knew what NOT to do. As soon as the tire blew out I immediately took my foot off the gas pedal (I did not brake) and grabbed the steering wheel FIRMLY because the van was trying to pull toward the missing tire. Once I knew I had the vehicle under control, I made sure the shoulder on the right was clear and eased the van onto the shoulder. Now I GENTLY braked to bring the van to a stop a SAFE distance away from the interstate traffic. As I wiped the sweat from my brow, I heard one of my golfers say, "Man, that was cool!" If that was so cool, why was I sweating? I hate to think what might have happened if I had not been a driver education teacher because I knew exactly what to do and not to do when this tire blowout occurred.

Brake Failure – If your foot brake fails, do the following:

1. Quickly pump the brake pedal 3 or 4 times to try to restore brake fluid pressure.
2. If this doesn't work, shift to a lower gear. This downshifting will help slow the vehicle.
3. Use the parking brake for the final stop.
4. Be sure you are ready to steer at any time to avoid a collision.

Engine Failure – If your engine dies while you are driving, do the following:

1. Carefully shift to Neutral and try to restart the engine.
2. If this doesn't work, put on your emergency flashers to let others know your vehicle is in trouble.

3. Keep in mind, since you do not have engine power, you will not have power steering or power brakes, so be sure not to go off the road or try to turn left or right too fast.
4. After safely exiting the roadway, make sure your vehicle is a safe distance away from traffic.
5. Get a safe distance away from your vehicle and traffic and call for help.

Stuck Accelerator – If your accelerator sticks, do the following:

1. Kick at the accelerator a couple of times with your right foot.
2. If this doesn't work, I would shift to Neutral and brake.
3. Be prepared to steer to avoid a collision.

Passing Another Vehicle (Two-way Highway vs. Interstate)

Passing another vehicle on a two-way highway was one of the most difficult skills to teach because it was rare for us to approach a vehicle on a rural highway that was going slow enough for us to be able to pass. According to our textbook, ALL PASSING MUST BE DONE WITHIN THE SPEED LIMIT. Our textbook also advised that if you are passing, you should travel at least 10 mph faster than the vehicle you are passing, (which I completely agree with) so you could clear the oncoming lane as soon as possible. It was very rare for us to approach a vehicle traveling at 45 mph or less, unless it was some type of farm equipment. Our textbook also recommended whenever you are thinking about passing a vehicle on a 2-way road you should definitely answer yes to the following three questions:

1. Is it safe? Certainly, this should be the most important consideration. Sometimes you

will be on a two-way highway without a no passing sign or solid yellow line on your side of the road but it still may not be a safe place to pass. You may not have enough sight distance ahead (especially for an inexperienced driver), or there may be an intersection ahead. Keep in mind it is illegal to pass at or near an intersection.

2. Is it legal? Remember, it is not legal to drive over the speed limit even when passing, but if I were passing a vehicle that was traveling 50 mph, I would accelerate to at least 60 mph to clear the oncoming lane. Of course, it is not legal to pass in a marked no passing zone (solid yellow line on your side of the road), or when a hill or curve obstructs your view, but I think the most difficult problem to identify is an intersection ahead. These intersections may or may not be marked with an intersection sign ahead. As you can tell, it is very difficult to find rural highways that have a lot of areas that are safe and legal for your driver to practice.

3. Is it worthwhile? Will passing the vehicle ahead of you on a two-way highway really save a lot of time? I can't tell you how many times our driver education car was passed shortly before entering a town (sometimes this pass was not done safely either) and as we approached a four-way stop in town, we were right behind the vehicle that passed us. But the passing that really annoyed me was when another driver would pass us on a rural highway and a short time later would put on a left turn signal. Now we would have to slow down for the vehicle that just passed us. Several times after this "selfish" pass, this vehicle that was now turning left would have to stop because of oncoming traffic so now we had to STOP behind a vehicle that just passed us! Talk about a "Pet Peeve"!

Following is our textbook procedure for passing another vehicle on a two-way highway:

1. Move from your following distance (3 or more seconds) to your ready position, which is 2 seconds behind the vehicle you intend to pass. (I think it is very important for your driver to leave enough room to pull back in behind the vehicle ahead of you if he/she identifies an oncoming vehicle as he/she starts to pass.)

2. When it is safe to pass, signal left to prepare for your lane change, and check over your left shoulder to make sure no vehicles are in your blind spot. (I also think your driver should check their mirrors, because several times I had a student driver preparing to pull into the left lane, and then see some "inconsiderate driver" behind us had already started to pass us. This usually happened when we were trying to pass farm equipment since it was so difficult for the student driver to see around these vehicles.
3. Change lanes smoothly and accelerate at least 10 mph faster than the vehicle you are passing. However, all passing should be done within the speed limit.
4. Make a final evaluation. Provided you have not passed the vehicle, you can change your mind if any conflicts to your front zone exist 20-30 seconds ahead. If your front zone is clear, continue to accelerate to proper speed. Remember, many young drivers, including my son, have difficulty accelerating while lane changing. This could make it more difficult for your driver to pass the vehicle quickly enough.
5. Maintain your speed until you can see at least one of the headlights of the vehicle you are passing in your rearview mirror.

6. Signal for a right lane change, and return smoothly to the right lane. Do not slow down.
7. Cancel your turn signal and adjust your speed and lane position.

Other thoughts about passing another vehicle:

If possible, I think it would be best for most drivers to get some practice passing on an interstate or four-lane road before attempting a pass on a two-way highway. On a four-lane highway, you normally don't have to worry about oncoming traffic but you could still have intersections ahead. Even though you now should not have to worry about oncoming traffic, you should still follow the seven steps mentioned above, especially being able to accelerate at least 10 mph faster than the vehicle you are passing.

When we were discussing passing in the classroom I used to tell my students, "Wouldn't it be great if we had two driver education cars at Wesclin so we could practice passing each other." This usually got a big laugh from the class. Then I told them that I was serious and we had a perfect highway to try it on. It was an express highway (no town traffic), had a great sight distance just like an interstate, and had wide paved shoulders on both sides of the road. If you have access to two vehicles, you may want to think about this plan. However, I still think it would be a good idea for your driver to have some passing experience on a four-way highway or interstate first.

Whenever you driver is attempting a pass, especially on a two-way highway, remember the primary rule for deciding whether or not to turn at an intersection works just as well in this situation, "IF YOU DON'T KNOW, DON'T GO!"

Another major problem while attempting to teach passing is the fact the experienced driver is sitting on the right side of the car while the student driver has to check the lane to the left. Please remember to keep a safe distance behind the vehicle being passed so your driver will have enough room to pull back into the right lane if it is determined that it is not a safe place to pass. As you can tell, this was not one of my favorite maneuvers to accomplish with my students. Again, the biggest problem was not being able to see oncoming traffic and possible hazards before my student driver did.

The Basic Speed Law (or should it be the Common Sense Law)?

Can you name the 3 situations where you can be ticketed (driving too fast) for driving the posted speed limit? When I asked this question to my class here were two of the most popular (incorrect) answers. These were good thoughts but not the correct answers.

In a construction zone – This is not the case since most all construction zones have POSTED speed limit signs for safe driving.

In a school zone – This is also not the case since school zones are also marked with speed limit signs for when it is a school day and children are present.

Have you gotten the 3 correct answers without looking them up on your phone? Here we go!

1. In any type of bad weather – this includes

rain, snow, freezing rain (Yikes!) and my least favorite – Fog!

2. In heavy traffic – Luckily, I did not have to drive very often in rush hour traffic, but I always seemed to notice someone weaving in and out of traffic trying to beat everyone to work.
3. In residential areas where children are playing – We did not face this situation very often since most children who may have been playing near the streets were in school when we were behind the wheel.

I think the most difficult thing about the Basic Speed Law for your young driver is determining what is the "SAFE" speed for these situations. I think it would be much safer for your inexperienced driver to err on the side of caution and drive a little slower than you or I might.

For example, if it is raining, how much should your driver slow down? Of course, we know that the harder it is raining the more we need to slow down. But I always told my classes, if you have to use your high-speed wipers, you need to slow down a lot! Keep in mind the more severe the rainstorm the easier it might be to hydroplane, and I believe the most important thing a driver can do to prevent hydroplaning is to control their speed on wet roads.

What You Should Do When It Is Raining Cats and Dogs

I still remember driving with my family on vacation when it was raining very heavily. We were on the interstate and it was so difficult to see that I was only traveling 25 to 30 mph. I don't like the idea of pulling to the shoulder in this situation since it so difficult for the other drivers to see you parked. My plan was to take the next exit and get off the interstate until the rain slowed down. Luckily, after 5 minutes or so (which felt more like 5 hours), the rain began to subside and I was able to increase my speed because of the improved visibility. Several hours later when we got to our hotel to spend the night, we found that our clothes hanging in the back of the van (which was only a year or two old) were soaked from the rain! I guess it must have been raining sideways!

If you are driving during a snow storm, the two biggest concerns will be how much snow has accumulated on the road and your visibility. Adjust your speed depending on the severity of each. Hopefully, the first time you drive with your son/ daughter you will wait until the storm is over so their major concern will be the snow packed roads. I believe when you are driving on snow packed roads you will need to perform three skills very carefully – braking, steering and accelerating. At school, we would not cancel behind the wheel lessons for snow packed roads. In fact, driving on snow packed roads was one of my favorites! The only two elements in which I would not drive with students were possible freezing rain and very thick fog.

When driving in fog I think it all depends on your level of visibility. I have driven in some fog that was so light that I drove at the speed limit. But I have also driven in some "pea soup" fogs where I was driving about 20 mph on the highway. I think you should always be prepared to stop within your field of vision. Hopefully, you can practice with your driver the unenviable task of driving in the fog several times before he/she gets their license.

After having thought about it, freezing rain might be the worst! Not knowing when rain will actually start freezing is the biggest problem. Remind your driver when the temperature falls toward 32 degrees, the bridges and overpasses will usually freeze first! This happens because air under the overpass or bridge cools more quickly than the ground under the roadway. The vehicle I currently drive gives me a reminder about potential freezing when the temperature reaches 37 degrees. So also remind your driver that it doesn't have to fall to 32 degrees for roadways to start freezing.

What You Should Do In Heavy Traffic

When driving in multi-lane rush hour traffic, it will be almost impossible to keep a safe following distance because as soon you think you have it, someone will most likely change lanes in front of you. Of course you will want your driver to try to drive with the flow of traffic which during rush hour is usually below the speed limit. Try not to follow a vehicle that is bigger than the one you are driving, so you can identify several vehicles ahead. That way, if you see brake lights ahead, you can be ready to slow or stop without endangering the vehicle directly in front of you.

What You Should Do When Children Are Playing

When driving in residential areas where children are playing, not only is it important to be driving a safe speed (under the speed limit), I think it is vital your driver cover the brake as much as possible. If a child does run, walk, bicycle, skateboard, or roller skate out in front of your vehicle, your driver will be ready to brake and possibly steer and not hit the gas pedal by mistake. You may want to have your driver in a residential area "without children" drive at 10 or 15 mph and practice covering the brake for 10 seconds or so to see how much the vehicle will or won't slow. As long as you are not driving uphill, most vehicles we had in driver education would continue between 10 and 15 mph for a long time! Therefore, you can drive through most residential areas with your foot over the brake while you try to identify all possible hazards and just as importantly predict the worst. Remember, you don't want your driver to collide with another "Little Mr. Hund!"

As your driver gains experience, I think it is very important both you and your young driver agree you are always following the Basic Speed Law by driving at truly safe speeds when you encounter bad weather, heavy traffic or areas where children are playing.

One final question – As a driver, which do you think is worse, having bad traction or bad visibility? Most of my students felt it was bad traction but I disagree. Whenever I am driving the situation I hate most is not being able to identify possible hazards a safe distance ahead. I feel when your traction is bad (except for potential freezing rain) you just need to slow to a safe speed for the conditions. The next time you drive in a pouring rain storm or thick fog, you might agree.

Left and Right Turns – Not So Easy For A Beginner

When first practicing left and right turns with your beginning driver, keep in mind how many turns you have made in your driving career. I would bet for most of you it would be a hundred thousand or more. Many beginning drivers will have no idea when to start turning and when to start counter steering to complete the turn. You and I don't have to think about the physical part of making a right or left turn. I think the best place you can start making turns with your inexperienced driver is a vacant parking lot. I recommended to our students they could use the High School parking lot on most Saturdays or Sundays for their first drive. This would allow them to make turns with a lot of extra space and with little or no traffic.

I am not a big fan of taking your son/daughter on a back road (in class we defined this as a rural road with no lane markings and usually no speed limit signs). The main problems with backroads: many are narrow, bumpy, have loose gravel on the sides and also at intersections. It would be difficult and possibly frightening for your inexperienced driver to meet oncoming traffic. They also have many sharp curves or turns (15 mph or less) and some may not have a warning sign prior to the change of direction. Remember back road driving means about half the year, your driver will be dealing with corn or even bean fields that can totally obstruct their view at intersections. Because of the higher speeds, difficulty with sight distance and possible loss of traction, I do not recommend using backroads for your child's first drive.

Each year at my school, we practiced driving with about 100 students. Each year, we averaged 10-20 students that had never driven before their first time behind the wheel of the driver education car. Since it was a school day, we were not able to use the school parking lot, so we improvised. Luckily, we had a large block at a nearby park that was almost the same as a parking lot for a student's first drive. If I had two very inexperienced drivers for our first behind the wheel session, I would drive the students to the park. I certainly did not want my driver's first left turn to be on a highway with a speed limit of 55 mph. This site was tremendous for left turns since the roads were extremely wide, we had great sight distances as we approached each intersection and most importantly, we faced little or no traffic. As our first-time drivers made their left and right turns, I reminded them that it is fine to take these turns slowly, the last thing we wanted was a driver to attempt a turn too fast! For the student's first few turns, I wanted them only to concern themselves with steering into the turns and properly counter steering to complete the turn. As my beginner got more comfortable, then we worked on proper lane position for each turn.

You Can't Take Anything for Granted

This example occurred during my first week of my first year as a driver education teacher. Cindy, who had never driven before, was attempting her first left turn after I had driven her and her driving partner to town. As we approached the intersection, Cindy started turning at the proper time but what she did next proved to me that some beginning drivers know almost nothing about driving a car! As Cindy should have started counter steering, she did nothing; she did not attempt to straighten the wheels at all. Since we were on an even surface and no other traffic was approaching, I had Cindy approach the intersection with her foot covering the brake. Thank goodness! I used my brake and reached over to help her straighten the vehicle but we had already crossed over to the other lane. After this horrendous left turn, I had Cindy pull to the right side of the road and park for a short time. I then asked her why she did not straighten the wheels to finish the turn and she told me, "I thought the car would straighten out by itself."

I remember telling this story several years later to a fellow driver education teacher and of course he said, "I have a better one then that!" He had a student on his/her first drive and as they approached a four-way intersection he asked the driver to make a right turn. So, the student put on a right turn signal and proceeded straight across the intersection. When he asked the student why he/she did not begin steering he/she said, "I thought when I put on the signal, the car would turn on its own." I believe these two stories convinced me that when teaching in the classroom and behind the wheel to never take for granted the extent or lack of a student's knowledge.

For your child's first drive, if possible, I would begin with left turns. Even though they are more dangerous in traffic, I believe they are much easier for a novice to perform. When turning left you don't have to turn until you're near the center of the intersection and you don't have to steer or counter steer as sharply as you do for a right turn. When making a right turn you must be much more precise about exactly when to start your turn and when and how much to counter steer to complete this maneuver. Our speed limit for a left or right turn in the driver education car was 15 mph but of course many turns should be made at much lower speeds. I only allowed a 15 mph turn when we were turning off a main road and onto an area with excellent sight distance and no potential hazards ahead (certainly not into a driveway or crowded parking lot). After you feel your driver has become proficient at physically turning left and right (first time drivers had more difficulties with right turns), I would recommend driving on some side streets in town (20-25 speed limit). Be patient with your beginning driver if he/she is not comfortable with turning if there is a vehicle in the other lane, even if it is several blocks away.

Your driver will also need to perform turns from stop signs, yield signs and while moving when he/she has the right of way and traffic is clear. I would suggest these first turns be completed at 10 mph or less so your driver does not feel rushed. One of my favorite lines in our textbook is be sure to "build your experience gradually". Keep in mind since you are now on a public road (no longer a vacant parking lot), you will have to work with your driver at identifying all possible hazards such as moving vehicles, parked vehicles, bike riders and pedestrians. At this point, I think you should be very vocal about these potential hazards because I believe your driver will be so concerned with physically controlling the vehicle, they might not be ready to implement the IPDE System. After you both become comfortable with your driver's ability to complete these turns on side streets, I would have your driver practice turns onto the main road(s) of town. My more experienced first time drivers did this the first day but some of my very inexperienced drivers did not leave the park until they had driven two or three times. The two main roads in our town have speed limits of 35 mph, so as we prepared to join traffic, I made sure that our driver never felt that he/she had to hurry turning onto the highway. As we performed our first few right turns on to the main road, we made sure there was no traffic from either direction, just in case my driver was not able to stay in his/her lane throughout the turn.

By making sure there was no traffic from either direction, this allowed my driver to make a major steering error without a horrifying event. Accelerating properly when turning onto a road with a 35 mph speed limit was difficult for many of my drivers. When we left the high school (in a rural area) most of our drives started with a left or right turn onto the highway with a speed limit of 55 mph. I certainly did not want a beginning driver to have to deal with this situation until he/she proved they could join traffic in town successfully. After our drivers became proficient at turning on to highways at town speed, then we would practice left and right turns on to highways with 55 mph speed limits. Remember at 81 feet per second (this is 55 mph) or more, vehicles traveling on rural highways will need a lot of space if you are planning to enter their lane. You will also need a lot of space when turning left with a vehicle approaching in the nearest lane. With very inexperienced drivers, I would not ask them if they were going or waiting; I would talk with them about whether or not we had a safe gap in which to turn. I felt it worked best to talk more with a beginner and as they gained more experience, I gave them more control of the decision making process. Another thing to keep in mind is that we all learn certain skills at a different pace. Please try to be patient with your child if he/she has difficulties with what most drivers consider to be an easy skill.

My First Drive – Way to Go, Dad!

The first time my dad took me driving, he didn't take me to a parking lot...he took me to the cemetery. We had very little or no traffic, but we did not have much room to make turns. I had successfully completed a few turns and started to feel like I knew what I was doing. This feeling didn't last long!

While attempting a right turn in our full-sized pickup truck, I was faced with two concrete posts on both sides of the road (this rock road was about the size of an alley). As a complete beginner, I thought everything would be fine as long as I did not strike one of these concrete posts with the front of the truck. I certainly did not know that when making a right turn the front of the vehicle and the back of the vehicle do not take the same path. I wonder how many of you have hit the back tire of a curb when making a very sharp right turn. I can still hear that eerie sound of the back of the truck scraping along the concrete post on one of my first right turns. I also remember my dad saying that this collision was his fault because he should not have had me driving in such tight spaces. But I still got a hard time from my older brothers who told me that they were never going to ride with me. For a driver who wrecked a vehicle on his first drive what else would you become when you grew up but a driver education teacher!

Approaching Railroad Crossings – Always Be Prepared to Stop!

One of my favorite lines about railroads comes from a film we used in class called "You Don't Know Tracks". The film emphasized that every time you are approaching a railroad crossing you should "EXPECT A TRAIN!" In fact, I found an article in our local newspaper that stated Illinois led the country in railroad crossing failures! This was defined as when the lights were not flashing and the gates were not down but there was actually a train approaching the railroad crossing. This was a scary statistic. I think it is critical to teach our young drivers to carefully approach every railroad crossing just like a yield sign. Always be prepared to stop a safe distance before the crossing. It does not matter if the crossing has warning lights or not – always expect a train! There will also be many obstacles such as trees, crops, buildings, houses etc. that prevent you from having a clear look at a potential oncoming train. Many times we had an actual railroad engineer come speak to our class and following are several things I learned:

1. It takes the average freight train about one mile to come to a complete stop. I always asked this question in class. Therefore, the train CANNOT stop for you.
2. Just as importantly, the train certainly cannot swerve!
3. When looking at an approaching train, even an experienced engineer cannot estimate how fast it is approaching.
4. The engineer is required to blow the horn as the train is approaching every crossing. Of course, those of us who live close to railroad tracks also know it does not matter what time of day. One time I asked an engineer if he knew how many crossings he had on his regular route. He said his regular route was across most of Indiana and Illinois and that he had 312 crossings. This meant he blew the horn 624 times for a round trip. When I was little (and even now) I thought it would be great to get to blow a train horn. After blowing the horn 624 times a day, I think the fun would wear off quickly.

I recall a day in driver education when we were approaching a railroad crossing with the lights flashing. However, the crossing did not have any gates blocking traffic from entering. We had a clear view and could easily identify a train approaching from the left. The student did a good job of braking early to prepare to stop. Suddenly the vehicle behind us not only passed, but raced across the tracks before the oncoming train. As we stopped a safe distance from the tracks and waited for the freight train to pass, I can still see the engineer of the train giving us a huge smile and a "double thumbs up" for safely waiting for the train to pass.

An engineer also told us in class that sometimes they have a state policeman ride the train with them and if someone "races" a train (crosses while the red lights are flashing) they can easily radio to a nearby trooper and catch the unsafe driver.

I also remember a day when I was driving my own car to a Wesclin football game and was driving on a backroad. Question: What is an uncontrolled railroad crossing? This is a crossing that should have a circular warning sign and a crossbuck sign at the actual tracks but has NO warning lights or gates. Since this was late August, the cornfields were fully grown. I consider myself a much better driver after teaching driver education because any safe driving maneuver I asked my students to perform should be what I do, as well. As I approached this unmarked crossing, I had my windows up, the air conditioning on, and the radio playing so I don't remember hearing the train whistle. But just as we did in the driver education car, I prepared to stop a safe distance from the crossing. I wonder what the chances were that a train would really be approaching at that time. Just as I was able to see around the cornfield on my left, I saw a freight train going very quickly. This was certainly startling. The only thing I should have done differently was to turn off the radio and open the windows since it was so difficult to identify the oncoming train. By doing this I would have heard the train whistle long before I got close to the actual crossing. No matter if the railroad crossing is controlled or uncontrolled, always be prepared to stop a safe distance from the railroad tracks!

The Number One Weakness of Driver Education Students

What do you think was the number one weakness of my driver education students behind the wheel? It didn't take much time to notice most of my drivers had a difficult time driving when the car was in reverse. I also believe this is a weakness for many experienced drivers. Why do you think this is so?

1. I think it is much more difficult to see what possible hazards are behind or beside you as you are backing up. Drive Right states that backing is a "high risk maneuver" because in most vehicles, "you cannot see the pavement within 45 feet to your rear". Backup cameras can certainly help with this problem, but make sure your driver does not rely only on a backup camera because he/she still needs to check all around the vehicle as he/she is backing. Before getting into your

vehicle it is a good idea to walk to the rear of the vehicle to make sure nothing is behind you before you start backing. Several years ago, before backup cameras, my wife backed out of our garage, and ran over my son's friend's bicycle that was lying on the driveway behind our van.

2. Most drivers are very inexperienced driving backward as compared to forward. In my classroom, I asked my students the following question, when using miles driven, what percentage does the average driver travel backward as compared to forward? Would you believe some of my students answered, 50 percent? The class average was usually about 20-25 percent! Then I gave them this example: Let's say you were going to a movie in O'Fallon and you backed out of your driveway. How many feet would you have been in reverse? We usually agreed about 20 feet. You then drove about 15 miles to arrive in O'Fallon. When you left the movie you backed up about 10 feet and drove another 15 miles home. So, you now have driven 30 feet backward and 30 miles forward. So, we multiplied 5280 feet X 30 = 158,400 feet forward compared to 30 feet backward. As you can see a normal driver will backup much less than 1% as compared to driving forward.

Another comparison to think about is how many times you drive backward and make a right or left turn as compared to the number of forward right and left turns. Because of this, many students had a difficult time knowing exactly when to start their backwards turn and exactly when to start counter steering to remain in the correct lane.

3. I also believe there are a lot of minor collisions in parking lots when at least one or both vehicles involved are in reverse. In Illinois, high school instructors are only required to drive with each student a minimum of 6 hours, so this is another important skill you will need to practice with your young driver. On the final exam, I had each driver back out onto a road to the right and to the left and each driver had to back up in a parking lot after performing an angle or perpendicular park. For each of these backing maneuvers, the student was graded on proper speed control, checking for traffic before they started backing, watching behind in the direction they were backing and quickly checking to all other corners of the vehicle and proper lane position. I still believe, even after passing the school driving exam, all my students needed **a lot more experience** driving in reverse.

Speed Control while backing – When I had my students backing, I wanted them to cover the brake, unless they had to back uphill. When backing uphill, I would have my student accelerate gently until they had enough momentum, then cover the brake to be prepared to stop. Once again, as my driver was preparing to stop, I did not want them to hit the gas pedal by mistake. This error could easily cause a collision.

Backing straight – When backing straight, I had my student put just their left hand at the top of the steering wheel and put their right arm over the passenger seat. As the driver backed up about 50-100 feet, he/she should have been watching where the car was going but was also required to make quick checks to the front and sides to be sure nothing had changed in the driving environment. For beginning drivers, I would recommend they do not accelerate but just cover the brake. You also need to make sure they know which way to steer to get the back of the car to go the proper direction. This maneuver is part of the Illinois Driver's License exam.

Backing and turning – Most of our practice backing and turning was from alleys where I had my students practice backing to the left and right onto a side street. When performing these maneuvers, I wanted my students to do the following:

After carefully turning into the alley or driveway, make a complete stop, shift to reverse and keep both hands on the steering wheel. This is not only better for steering control but this "allows easier head movement to check all four corners of the vehicle during the turn".

1. Back slowly with right foot over the brake pedal. If acceleration is needed, remind your driver to accelerate gently, then cover the brake.
2. Quickly check continuously to your right, left and behind for possible hazards. Be very careful to check not only for moving vehicles but for PARKED VEHICLES, BICYCLISTS OR PEDESTRIANS.
3. Try to start steering so you can back your vehicle into the correct lane. This may take extended practice!
4. As you begin to turn the wheel, watch the direction you are traveling and make quick checks to the front and sides of your vehicle. Continue this process and keep watching the direction you are backing until you make a complete stop.
5. As soon as you stop, SHIFT TO DRIVE, then assess the traffic around you.
6. If clear, accelerate gently and counter steer if needed.

When backing and turning make sure your driver watches over the correct shoulder. I had many students who were backing and turning left but watching over their right shoulder. If possible, you may want to start practicing backing and turning in an empty parking lot.

Driving on the Interstate

Statistically, driving on an interstate is much safer than a two-way highway for many reasons. Following are several reasons I always discussed in the classroom:

1. All traffic should be traveling the same direction but you may want to warn your young driver sometimes head-on collisions are caused by a driver losing control and crossing the median. Drivers taking the wrong ramp and traveling the wrong direction also sometimes happen. Many times these "wrong way" drivers are under the influence of illegal drugs or alcohol.
2. Even though there are no intersections, your driver needs to be aware of potential difficulties at entrance and exit ramps.
3. Driver has excellent sight distance
4. There are wide shoulders (especially on the right) if needed for an escape path
5. Drivers should not have to deal with slow moving vehicles, bicyclist or pedestrians

6. Many roadway signs help drivers in advance with finding the proper exit.

Despite these advantages your driver needs to know if there is a collision on the interstate, it could likely be severe because of the high speed and potential for multi-car collisions due to traffic.

Some of the difficulties (especially for inexperienced drivers) are as follows:

1. Higher speeds
2. More traffic
3. Interchanges – possible conflicts with vehicles that are merging or exiting
4. Construction zones – these can cause major slow-downs or possibly even complete stops
5. Lane changing – higher speeds and more traffic
6. More semi-trucks – many of my beginning drivers were frightened when we drove near semis
7. Traffic completely stopping – If there is a collision ahead, traffic can unexpectedly come to a complete stop

Remember to "Build your experience gradually". I think this phrase is especially true when it comes to practicing with your driver on the interstate.

Driving Can Be a Huge Mental Strain Especially for a Beginner

One of my favorite driving experiences for our son Tyler was a drive from Okawville to west St. Louis County. Tyler had driven the interstate close to 50 times before his first excursion to St. Louis. It was about a 60-mile drive on I-64 and I-70 which took about an hour. He started in light traffic which became moderate and finally heavy as we drove through St. Louis. For his first experience in heavy interstate traffic, I thought he did a great job. But I will never forget when Tyler pulled into a parking space and turned off the car, he let out a big sigh and announced, "I am not driving home!" I believe Tyler was not worn our physically from this drive, but I am sure he was "mentally tired". So, later I had to tease him, by saying, "If you drive over here with your friends sometime, are you going to call and have Mom or me drive you home?

Without a doubt, the most difficult part of interstate drives for our students was merging into traffic. I still remember one of the major points I learned about properly merging was to make sure you get your students to accelerate at or near the speed of the vehicles already on the interstate. I certainly agreed then and now, but following is what happened on the first merge we ever made in the driver education car.

A "Slight" Exaggeration

My driver Jeff had no experience merging on the interstate but the I-64 west merge ramp at New Baden was not usually very busy during school hours. As Jeff was about halfway up the entrance ramp, I was working with him on trying to "get up to speed". I was also able to check approaching traffic on the interstate. Luckily, we only had to deal with one vehicle, but of course it was a semi-truck. This semi was in the right lane (same lane we needed to merge into) and since there was no other traffic I thought the semi would change lanes to help us merge easier. But of course, the truck driver did not. Since it now looked like we were going to get to the merging area at about the same time as the semi I calmly told our driver to "slow down, slow down, slow down." Jeff braked gently, and we comfortably let the semi go first and merged after him. I still believe trying to "get up to speed" is important but this merge taught me the number one goal is to merge safely. Later that day, one of Jeff's other classroom teachers asked me, "What happened in the driver education car this morning? Jeff said you missed a semi by AN INCH!" I told her we missed the semi by at least 100 feet. So, if you ever meet Jeff, you may not want to believe how big the fish was that got away!

Luckily My Observer Was Not Driving!

One of the most startling merges we ever had took place at the O'Fallon/Scott Air Force Base "cloverleaf" on Interstate 64. My driver Kevin was 6' 6" and was crammed into our little Chevy Prism. Since the entrance ramp is such a sharp curve (30 mph advisory speed limit), it was very difficult to "get up to speed" while preparing to merge. We also had some trees and bushes that did not allow us to get an early look at the approaching traffic on the interstate. About 2/3 of the way down the entrance ramp we were able to identify about 20-30 semi-trucks using both lanes of the interstate.

One of the main things I tried to teach my students was that EVERY TIME you attempt to merge, always check to see if you have an open shoulder in case traffic is so heavy you don't feel you can safely merge. The last thing you want to do is stop on an entrance ramp unless it is your only option. As Kevin approached the cloverleaf merge area (luckily none of the semis were planning to exit in the same area we were attempting to merge) we were traveling about 45 mph and I estimated the line of semis were going about 70 mph with very little space between them. Because of the semis, our little Prism was shaking, and our backseat student was whimpering. Luckily, Kevin was a "cool as the other side of the pillow" so I asked him to slow down gently and move to the shoulder on the right just past the cloverleaf exit lane. After the semis passed by, we were down to about 30 mph and when it was clear we finished our merge on to I-64. If the right shoulder would not have been clear we could have taken the exit ramp (the direction we did not want to go). Therefore, as your driver merges, be sure to always check the shoulder ahead to see if you have an escape path. This was an experience I shared with every class from then on. Merging on the interstate is not "a piece of cake"!

Merging in a construction zone – If you have the opportunity to merge in a construction zone with your driver – take advantage of it! This is a difficult maneuver because in a rural area there will be only one lane available and usually barricades are blocking the use of your shoulder as an escape path. What sign do you think should be at the bottom of your entrance ramp just before you will need to merge? It should be a yield sign and remember our definition of approaching a yield signs means you must be prepared to stop. This is the one situation where it may be a good idea to stop on a merge ramp. If you do have to stop on the merge ramp inside of a construction zone, it will now be difficult to merge on to the interstate since you now will have to pull out from a stopped position.

Exiting the interstate – Most of the interchanges in our rural area were diamond-shaped so exiting the interstate for us was not usually problematic. First, I had our driver identify the large green sign that told us of the exit ramp upcoming and be sure we were in the proper lane for the exit ramp. As we approached the exit, I made sure our driver properly signaled and did not slow down too soon. Since most of our diamond exit ramps had an advisory speed of 50 mph I would have our driver cover the brake as we got close to the exit. After we left the interstate my driver would gently brake to a safe speed to handle the exit ramp curve and prepare for the stop sign or traffic light at the end of the ramp. I did not want my driver going 50 mph or less before exiting in a 65 or 70 mph zone unless we had no other option.

Cloverleaf Ramp – The main purpose of a cloverleaf ramp is to allow vehicles to enter and exit the interstate without having to deal with an intersection at the end of the ramp. This allows the driver to exit the interstate or four-way highway and merge on to the next roadway. However, I feel there are two major difficulties when trying to enter or exit at a cloverleaf interchange. Can you think of one or both? At a cloverleaf interchange there are two potential entrance ramps and two exit ramps so if you choose the first ramp you will not have to deal with these two potential problems. When using the circular part of the cloverleaf interchange you will have to:

1. Prepare for a much lower advisory speed (30 mph or less on some ramps) on both the entrance ramp and exit ramp
2. a. When you are exiting you will have to prepare for vehicles that might be entering in the same area
   b. When you are entering you will have to prepare for vehicles that might be exiting in the same area

Exiting at a cloverleaf ramp – When preparing to exit at the "circular" part of a cloverleaf, I made sure my driver signaled right at the proper time (just after passing the diamond shaped first ramp) and:

1. IDENTIFY if any vehicles were preparing to merge in the same area we were exiting.
2. If vehicle(s) were on the entrance ramp, we needed to PREDICT who was going to arrive

at the "merging area" first. The exit would not be too difficult if we or the other vehicle(s) were clearly going to arrive first. But if we predicted we and the other vehicle(s) were going to arrive about the same time, we then had to make a very good DECISION about our speed and lane position.

3. If there were only one or two cars preparing to enter, then we would slow down gently and let them go first for two reasons. A– The cars that were merging needed to be able to accelerate "up to speed" so they could blend with traffic on the interstate. B– We needed to prepare for a 30 mph curve ahead so trying to accelerate to get ahead of one or two vehicles could lead to entering this sharp curve too fast. We certainly did not slow down to 30 mph when still on the interstate but usually slowed 5-15 mph to let the merging cars go first. Now for the fun part! If we identified three or more cars on the entrance ramp now we had to try to find a gap between them or behind them to find a safe place to fit when we approached the merging area. I usually had to help my driver in this situation not only find a safe gap but also the proper speed control to fit into that gap.

Diamond Ramp/ Cloverleaf Ramp - What's the Difference?

I remember an interstate drive many years ago with Randy, who as we walked toward the driver education car, told me that he had driven the interstate 20 or 30 times. But when I asked him if he had ever entered or exited at a cloverleaf interchange he said, "I don't think so, but it should be no problem." On our drive toward the interstate I reminded Randy that when you exit you will have to be ready for a 30 mph ramp and you will also have to be prepared to meet other vehicles in the same area. As we passed the first ramp and prepared to exit, there must have been 12-15 cars on the merge ramp and nobody left a safe gap for us to exit. They looked like a train – all connected at the bumper. What advice do you think I gave Randy? I said "Forget about the exit, if it is safe let's lane change to the left and go to the next exit." Once again, as a driver you have no control over what other drivers do! This story was then shared with every upcoming class to warn the students of the possible difficulty of exiting at a cloverleaf interchange. I also reminded the students if you ever identify the exit ramp ahead is overflowing and vehicles are stopped on the interstate, please try to make a safe lane change and go to the next exit. This ramp overflow could cause a violent rear end collision.

Another thing to watch for after your driver exits the interstate is a term our textbook called “velocitation”. This is defined as “after a driver has driven a long distance at high speed the driver may have difficulty with speed control after they exit the interstate”. Have your driver continuously check their speedometer after they exit to prevent a potential speeding ticket.

Tips for Driving on the Interstate – Some Things to Practice or Be Aware Of

1. Practice lane changing
2. Practice passing if possible (use same method as 2-way highway)
3. When traveling on a three or more lane interstate, be careful of changing toward the center lane(s) because a vehicle that is two lanes away could also be changing into the same lane
4. Be prepared to lane change at every merge
5. Do not pass at a merge (vehicle you are passing cannot lane change if someone is merging)

You Can't Sit Back and Relax!

What helped me more than anything was that no matter which student was driving (strong, average or weak), I pretended I was driving. By doing this, I felt I could always stay one step ahead of my student drivers to help prepare for the unexpected.

The first semester I taught behind the wheel I learned an extremely important lesson – Even my best drivers could make a MAJOR mistake.

Frank was leaving Shiloh on a two-way highway and approaching a median where the road was going to turn into a four-way road approaching a traffic light. What sign do you think was posted at the median ahead of us? It was a black and white "Keep Right" and my "good" driver started to gently steer to the left! I grabbed the top of the steering wheel and said "No, we need to go right." As we now went to the correct side of the "Keep Right" sign my driver said, "But I have never driven here before." My driver should have easily identified a median with a "Keep Right" sign so this was not a valid excuse. We know when your driver becomes licensed he/she is going to drive in a lot of places he/she has never been before. This lesson drove home the importance of not only seeing traffic signs, but also knowing what the signs mean.

I Was Completely Caught "Off-Guard"!

Probably the most unexpected maneuver by one of my drivers occurred in Aviston. Sarah was driving on one of the main streets in town with a speed limit of 30 mph when I asked her to turn right at the next intersection. She pushed the turn signal upward (I would estimate that when a student put on the wrong turn signal I noticed this error 99% of the time) so as Sarah slowed to a safe speed for her right turn – She turned left! This would not have been such a big mistake except we had an oncoming car bearing down on the right side of our car. Without thinking, I said firmly but without yelling, "hit the gas, hit the gas, hit the gas". Thankfully, Sarah was able to hit the gas pedal and avoid a possible side impact collision. This oncoming car was so close I thought this might be my "poop in my pants" moment.

I believe if Sarah would have mistakenly hit the brake instead, we would have been struck by the oncoming car. This collision could have resulted in serious injuries, especially for the student sitting behind me in the backseat or me. This was one of the only times we had a near collision that would have been the fault of my student driver and me. Keep in mind when your young driver has their permit, they most likely will be on your insurance policy, and as the parent, you will be mostly responsible for any errors behind the wheel.

After we completed this totally unexpected left turn, I asked my driver to pull over and parallel park on the right. After we discussed the fact she had put on a right turn signal then proceeded to turn left, she broke down in tears. She then told me about some major problem at home and felt this affected her concentration. I tried to comfort her but reminded her this was a major, not a minor, mistake. From this point on, I asked the students to let me know in advance if they were dealing with a problem that might affect their driving. I told them I would truly appreciate this because we could easily get a substitute driver and get them back on the driving schedule when they were emotionally ready. I don't think any inexperienced driver should be behind the wheel if they cannot give 100% focus to the driving task.

If You Are Not Careful, Danger Could Be Lurking on Rural Backroads

The final drive I took with most of my students was on some difficult backroads just north of Trenton. In class we defined rural backroads as roads in the country with no lane markings. The backroads we took on this final drive had the following potential problems:

1. Narrow
2. Poor Quality (Bumpy with loose gravel on sides and at intersections)
3. Hilly (Loss of sight distance)
4. No speed limit signs
5. Few warning signs for curves or turns ahead or sometimes the WRONG SIGN
6. Narrow concrete bridges (hitting one of these could be fatal or cause severe injury)
7. Animals – especially dogs on the loose
8. Corn or bean field blocking view at intersections

After gaining some experience with driving back roads with my students, I came up with four factors I think would be good for all drivers when determining a safe speed for driving on rural backroads:

1. What is the condition of the road? How rough or smooth is it? Is there a lot of loose gravel? How wide is the road? We drove some backroads that were almost as smooth and wide as a two-way highway, but we also drove some that were barely wide enough for two cars to meet.
2. What are the weather conditions? Remember the Basic Speed Law.
3. Are you driving at daytime or nighttime? At night it is going to be very difficult for you to see these upcoming curves and turns and remember some of them may or may not be marked with an advanced warning sign.
4. How well does the driver know the road?

Keep in mind most of these rural backroads will not have speed limit signs so it is totally up to the driver to choose a safe speed. I am a firm believer most wrecks on backroads involve only one car and if this is true it usually takes place because the driver was driving too fast for the conditions, unless an animal has intervened.

The Backroad Obstacle Course

Here is some information on the route we drove in the driver education car. After merging on to New Highway 50 north of Trenton we then turned left onto Crackerneck Road, our first rural backroad. About a half mile down Crackerneck Road we approached a four-way intersection. As we approached I asked the driver to tell me if the intersection ahead (Otter Road) was controlled or uncontrolled. Most students said it was uncontrolled. I told them no because Otter Road has two stop signs so we "should" have right of way. Can you imagine how dangerous a four-way uncontrolled intersection would be on a rural backroad especially if the crops are tall? I told the students that if you ever identify a real four-way uncontrolled intersection on a rural backroad you should call the police because someone may have stolen some stop or yield signs.

Next, we approached a steep hill on a narrow road. Many times I had to tell my student to slow down and move to the right as we approached this hill just in case we were to meet an oncoming vehicle near the crest of the hill. Remember – Predict the Worst!

About a mile later we approached a right turn sign, indicating a 90 degree turn. Since most of my drivers had no experience on this backroad, I reminded them we have to be prepared for a 15 mph or less sharp turn. As we got into the actual right turn most of my drivers found out that this was not as sharp as the sign indicated. But I reminded them it is a lot safer approaching a turn or curve a little too slow instead of a little too FAST! After completing the right curve which was not as sharp as the sign indicated, we approached a left turn ahead sign and just like the turn before it was not as sharp as the sign indicated. About a quarter of a mile later I had the driver turn left onto Rutz Road. After the turn I asked the driver how they liked or didn't like Rutz road. Most but not all of my drivers immediately noticed this road was much narrower than Crackerneck. Just ahead we approached a hill we could not see over and we were on a very narrow road. Again, I had to tell many drivers to slow down in case we meet a car near the approaching hill because we might have to leave the road and drive in the loose gravel or grass on the right.

Next, we approached a yield sign at a 4-way intersection with Sportsmen's Road. It was very difficult to identify cross traffic at this intersection so I made sure the driver was "ready to stop!" As we drove straight ahead our driver faced two slight hills but they still blocked our vision of oncoming traffic. By now, most of my drivers were slowing properly and moving to the right just in case. As we approached the second hill, I asked my driver to tell me as soon as we can see past the second hill and to let me know which way the road ahead changes direction (thankfully it was daytime driving). Soon after the driver got over the second hill we could identify that the road was going to the left but there was no advanced (yellow) warning sign and to make it even more dangerous this was not a curve but an "Unmarked Left Turn". This turn was even more difficult when we had a cornfield on our left as we approached. I made sure the driver was prepared to make this "blind" left turn at nearly 10 mph. After this left turn we then approached another steep downhill situation so again I asked if they knew which way the road was going at the bottom of the hill. This time it was an unmarked right curve, but it was very difficult to see around so not only did I want the student to be driving a safe speed, I wanted them to have their right foot over the brake.

Here are the three most memorable events we had at this sharp downhill right curve with a very limited sight distance.

1. We once met a man picking up trash along the right side (our lane) of the road so with our foot over the brake and driving a safe speed we would have been able to stop safely but since there was no oncoming car my driver was able to gently steer to the left, to minimize the hazard.
2. It was a beautiful spring day and as my driver started into this right curve we met a woman pushing a baby stroller on the right side of the road. Just like in situation #1, since we had our speed under control and foot over brake my driver could easily steer around the baby stroller.
3. This one was more startling than the first two. Just as we approached the end of the curve we identified two men who were standing in the middle of the road (bikes beneath them) and each one of them had a dog on a leash! This time we were not able to steer around them, so my driver and I had to make a complete stop!

Of course, most of the days we drove around this dangerous curve we did not face the "unexpected" but remember we always needed to cover the brake and predict the worst!

The next problem we faced ahead was a small unmarked (except for some orange paint) one lane concrete bridge without a warning sign. Of course this bridge would be much more difficult to identify at night. Believe it or not, just after we crossed this bridge, there was a yellow diamond warning us of a "narrow bridge" but there was not a warning of the sharp left turn to enter this "Large" concrete bridge and the right turn that was needed as soon as you crossed this concrete bridge. Now for the final problem on this backroad "obstacle course". About a half mile later we approached a yellow warning sign for a left curve with no advisory speed so I asked my driver, "What do you think would be a safe speed for this upcoming curve?" Most of my students said either 25 or 30 mph but quite a few said 40-45 mph. Shockingly, this was not a left curve it was a "full left turn," so I usually had to tell my driver to slow down and be prepared for 10-15 mph. If a driver entered this turn at 30 mph or more I am not sure he/she could have avoided loss of control of the vehicle.

I hope this final drive I took students on can help you when teaching your young driver about the many hidden dangers of rural backroad driving. I hope we can convince our inexperienced drivers it is okay to drive a little too slow when facing new situations but especially on unfamiliar rural backroads at night.

"An Excellent Driver Never Stops Learning"

This is a line I borrowed from the author of our textbook and turned it into a classroom bulletin board. Each semester the students were required to find at least five articles pertaining to driver education. The students were also responsible for writing a brief summary of what he/she learned from reading the articles. Students were not supposed to tell me about the facts of the article but what they learned from reading it. Also, each student had to find at least one article that was not about a collision. Following are some topics of the eye-opening articles my students found:

- Two off-road recovery incidents – one driver overcorrected and hit two oncoming motorcycles and one driver overcorrected and lost control. Both of these incidents had fatalities.
- A 20-year-old, with only an instruction permit and while driving unsupervised, swerved to avoid a bicycle and crashed through a

fence. The driver survived a 30-foot drop onto railroad tracks.

- Two people were killed on a backroad in a one-car collision when neither occupant was wearing a seatbelt. Both were thrown from the vehicle and police did not know who was driving.
- A man was shot by a police officer during a traffic stop when he reached for a cane in the bed of the truck. I stressed to my students that if you are stopped by a police officer, keep your hands on the steering wheel until the officer comes to your window and asks for your driver's license, registration, and possibly proof of insurance.
- Speed cameras increase safety – In a 20 mph zone before cameras were installed, drivers averaged 32 mph and 12 cars per hour were driving at 40 mph or more. After the cameras were installed, the average speed dropped to 18 mph and the speeders were being clocked in the low to mid 30's range rather than an aggressive 50 mph.
- Can you be liable if you are texting someone you know is driving at the time? This article was from a crash that happened about ten years ago but the case is not yet settled.

- During my last year of teaching, three students found three different articles about drivers who were killed or seriously injured while performing U-turns, which many people would consider a "simple" maneuver.

Distracted Driving

One of the major changes I saw as a driver education teacher was the profound increase in the possible distractions for the driver of a motor vehicle. Our textbook (copyright 2000) did not even mention distracted driving in the index. However, the updated version (copyright 2010) had a whole chapter devoted to the dangers of distracted driving. As of 2019, what do you think are by far the two greatest distractions for a licensed teenage driver?

Some of the common distractions while driving include the following:

- Eating and drinking
- Grooming or applying makeup
- Reading or writing
- Changing music
- Reaching for an object

However, the two greatest distractions are cell phone usage (especially texting) and other passengers in the vehicle.

According to a study by the Virginia Tech Transportation Institute, texting while driving is the functional equivalent of a drunk driver and is twenty-three times more likely to be involved in an accident or near collision. A study by Car and Driver magazine states that a texter is a significantly greater threat than a drunk driver.

Study: Teen Driver death rate rises with number of passengers

16 year old – one passenger up 39%, two up 86% and three or more 182%

17 year old – one passenger up 48%, two up 158% and three 207%

Without a doubt 16 and 17 year old drivers are safest when driving by themselves.

A Few More of My Favorite Stories

And Your Dad is a What?

Many years ago Shari was on her final drive after she had already passed her driving exam, and was on a 4-lane highway approaching a traffic light. I asked Shari to make a right turn on red at the next intersection and here is what she did. Shari used her right turn signal at the proper time and braked smoothly as we approached the traffic light. As we neared the intersection she did an excellent job of checking for potential hazards to her left, right, front and behind. After completing a smooth right turn there was only one thing Shari forgot to do, she did not make a complete stop! But she did slow down to about 2-3 mph so this was a safe but not "legal" turn.

When we were safely on I-64 driving toward New Baden and Shari was now in the back seat (her partner was driving back), I asked Shari if she would do me a favor. I asked her to ask her dad who was a state policeman what he would do if he saw a vehicle make a right turn on red and the driver did a good job of slowing as he/she approached, used their signal properly and did an excellent job of checking for traffic but the driver didn't quite make a complete stop! Immediately Shari said, "Oh, Mr. Hund, I thought I got away with it!" I said, "It is okay that your turn wasn't perfectly legal but it sure was safe. No, really, please ask your dad what he would do if he saw a vehicle (in moderate traffic) not quite make a complete stop." When I saw Shari at school the next day she told me "He would 'nail' you!" Try to work with your young driver to be sure the front end of the car gently rocks back so you know you have made a complete stop. This only takes a couple more seconds, but this gives you a little extra time to be sure the intersection is clear before completing a right turn on ted.

When Faced With an Imminent Collision, Never Give Up!

Years ago, the high school baseball team qualified for the state tournament in Joliet which was about a 5 hour drive. Instead of a school bus, we rented a small (rectangular seating) bus for the trip north. The coaches and I were the "lucky" ones who got to sit with our backs facing the direction we were going. We were on a two-way highway about 30 minutes into our trip when suddenly I felt something was wrong (since seated backwards I could not see what was going on in front of us). Our bus driver was braking very hard for a second or two then swerved to the left and began to accelerate. Suddenly, our driver swerved to the right and "BANG" we hit something and continued to the right shoulder of the highway and stopped. The first thing the coaches and I did was to make sure the players on the bus were okay. We had a couple of broken cell phone screens, but everyone seemed to be all right.

Here is what happened. Our bus was following a pickup truck pulling a horse trailer and this vehicle was planning on turning right on Fruit Road. I'm not positive if the right turn signal was working on the trailer or not. There was also a pickup truck on Fruit Road to the right and the driver of the pickup with horse trailer probably did not think he had enough room for this right turn so he slowed firmly or possibly stopped on the highway. At this point the driver of our bus felt he would not be able to stop without rear ending the horse trailer so after identifying the left lane of the highway was clear, he steered into the left lane and began to accelerate.

At this moment, the driver of the pickup truck on Fruit Road proceeded to pull into the intersection right in front of our charter bus (and remember our driver had just started to accelerate to pass the horse trailer). One of my favorite lines in the driver's education textbook was whenever you are faced with a possible collision "ABOVE ALL, DO NOT GIVE UP, any change of speed or direction that lessens the impact will help." At the last second our bus driver was able to steer sharply to the right to strike the pickup truck in the bed instead of the door frame. I truly believe this last second maneuver saved the pickup truck driver from either severe injury or possibly even death. I heard the reason the pickup truck driver pulled out in front of our bus was that he DIDN'T SEE us. I think this happened because he was totally focused on the truck with the horse trailer and knew he didn't have enough room to make this right turn. But this is a perfect example of what can happen if you STARE at something in the traffic scene instead of getting the "big picture."

Be sure that when your young driver is waiting at an intersection he/she keeps their EYES MOVING so they won't pull out in front of a vehicle that they did not see. Luckily our driver worked for another bus company so about 2 hours later we were able to get a replacement bus and get to the state tournament. Also, the driver of the pickup truck involved in the collision was pretty "shook up" but seemed to be physically okay. The pickup truck wound up on the left shoulder off of the highway.

Just Another Morning at Work?

For many years prior to the start of the school day I would get the Driver Education car out of the storage shed and drive it to the front of school. To accomplish this task, about an 800 foot distance, I needed to:

1. I backed the car in a straight line out of the shed toward the student parking area. As I was backing, I kept my foot over the brake and not only watched behind me but also quickly checked the sides and front and watched behind me until I made a complete stop.
2. As soon as I stopped, I shifted to drive and carefully steered slightly right around some parked cars.
3. Then I properly signaled, checked traffic and performed two right turns in the parking lot to prepare to stop at a yield sign at the end of the parking lot. I also was sure to signal left to prepare to leave the parking lot. I then checked very carefully for cross traffic on Wesclin Road (a three-way intersection) because many students and teachers used this entrance.
4. I performed a safe left turn on to Wesclin Road (rural back road) and prepared to stop at the stop sign at Highway 160 (speed limit of 55 mph). I then signalled for a left turn

onto the highway. There was no stop line, crosswalk or sidewalks so I made sure to stop a safe distance from the highway.

5. This was a four-way intersection with two stop signs for drivers on Wesclin Road. Since this was about 20-30 minutes before the start of school there was usually a lot of traffic. Now I needed to find a safe gap to make this left turn. After turning onto Highway 160 I only need to go about 500 feet before the entrance to the high school, so I put on my turn signal immediately.
6. Once I got to this point, I identified about 6-8 oncoming cars on Highway 160. I felt I was going to have to stop for them and I also identified I DID NOT have a vehicle in front of me. As I slowed down and prepared to stop, I checked my rearview mirror and identified a vehicle approaching FAST. Remember I could not safely turn left because of oncoming traffic. What should I do to prevent a potential rear end collision? Easy!! I just took my foot off the brake and hit the gas pedal and went FORWARD. Just as I started forward I heard the brakes of the car behind me squeal. I felt the key to avoiding this possible collision was not totally focusing on the oncoming vehicles but having the GOOD HABIT of checking my mirrors.

7. After avoiding this potential collision, I just drove another 500 feet or so and turned into the middle school parking lot. Next, I drove around the perimeter of this parking lot to get back to the highway. Once again, I signaled and checked traffic for each turn.
8. After turning right out of the middle school parking lot I was able to safely turn right into the high school parking lot.
9. Then I used my left turn signal, checked my mirrors again and since this time it was clear I safely turned into the Wesclin Driver Education car parking spot.

   *** A reminder that for every maneuver in the high school or middle school parking lot I was very alert for potential pedestrians (students or parents). I had my foot over the brake as much as possible while driving in both parking lots.

Once again, this was something that seemed so easy. I drove the car from the shed to our parking spot every school day until this "close call". From then on, after backing the driver ed car out of the shed, I then parked the car in the school parking lot near the vocational building so the students and I got a little more exercise for our first driving lesson of the day.

Please take a good look at steps 1-6 and 9 (not 7 or 8 because I usually didn't have to use the middle school parking lot). What seemed like a routine driving route for me would not be an "easy" drive for a novice driver. I had to:

1. Back out into possible traffic (student parking area)
2. Drive around the student parking lot and be prepared for other vehicles or pedestrians at every turn before reaching the parking lot exit.
3. Make a left turn onto Wesclin Road with possible students or teachers entering the parking lot from left or right.
4. Make sure to find a "safe gap" for a left turn onto a busy highway with some students or teachers turning left or right onto Wesclin Road.
5. Make a left turn off the highway into a busy high school parking lot.
6. Make a safe left turn in the parking lot into the Wesclin Driver Education car parking space.
7. Finally, after leaving the car, I now needed to be a "safe" pedestrian to enter school.

Entering a Semi-Truck's Blind Spot – A Real Danger Zone

About 20 years ago, I was driving Interstate 64 in a rural area on my way home from Nashville, Illinois. About 5 miles after merging, I approached a semi-truck I was preparing to pass on the left. At this time, the speed limit was 65mph and the semi's was 55 mph. When I was approaching the semi driver's side door(definitely in his blind spot), the driver put on his left turn signal, YIKES! What do you think I did when I identified this turn signal?

1. First, I knew that I had an escape path to the left, but that would mean possibly taking my car off the road into the grass median. But this would be better than being run over by a semi!
2. I BLARED the horn and braked gently just in case he started to lane change and I might have to steer toward the grass median.
3. Thankfully, the horn got the driver's attention

because he started to move slightly to the left and then steered back to the right lane.

4. Whew!!! I am glad I didn't have to steer off the road in to the grass median.

Be sure your young driver truly understands that the horn is a SAFETY DEVICE!

A Difference of Opinion

Many years ago, Karen was taking her final driving exam when this took place. We were on two-way highway about a mile and a half from Trenton with a 55 mph speed limit and approached a "makeshift" construction zone. This construction zone did not have any signs or flashing light for a reduced speed limit and it consisted of two men and a pickup truck. As we approached, the two men were on one side of the highway and their truck was on the other. Since this was Karen's test I was not going to give any advice unless it was absolutely necessary. As Karen approached, she started to smoothly brake to what I thought was a safe speed. Just then one of the workers started walking toward the highway and proceeded to cross the road. Karen was able to brake firmly (but the Anti-Lock Brakes did not "kick in") and was easily able to avoid the construction worker "pedestrian." When the driving exam was over I asked Karen the same question I usually asked every driver, "Was there anything you wished you would have done differently?" Immediately Karen said, "I can't believe that man just walked right out if front of me. I wish I would have been going slower."

At the bottom right corner of my test page I noted how well I thought she had handled the construction worker. The backseat observer also thought Karen did a good job with this situation. I think Karen did a good job of Identifying the potential hazards (2 men along side the highway), she Predicted something bad might happen, then Decided to brake gently and keep her foot on or above the brake as we approached and was able to correctly Execute by braking firmly when the construction worker crossed her path of travel. I think the reason she was so critical about the way she handled this pedestrian is that she really did not "Predict the Worst." But by braking early and keeping her foot on or over the brake pedal she was ready just in case!

In this situation I was covering the brake but did not have to hit the brake pedal because of the way Karen handled the situation. But in your car, you will not have an "instructor brake" so you will have to be even more cautious about possible braking situations. Proper use of the IPDE system can really help in these situations.

How Good Drivers Get Killed

Years ago, I stumbled across a copy of Reader's Digest that had this title on the front page: "How Good Drivers Get Killed". Immediately, I was curious to find out what the author of this article meant by a "Good Driver." The definition of a good driver in this article was a driver that was killed in a collision that was not his/her fault. I discussed this article in my classroom to teach my students they should not strive to just be a "good" driver – their goal should be to become an excellent driver.

Following are the top four types of collisions in which these drivers were killed:

1. Head on collision – I believe this is the most difficult to really predict but whenever you are driving a two-way highway you must always know if you have an escape path on your right and be prepared to use it!
2. Side impact collision at two-way stops – I believe this collision can either be avoided or at

least the severity lessened if your driver "covers the brake" or slows gently every time they approach an intersection with an oncoming vehicle (potential left turn) or a vehicle approaching from a side road. I think the real key here is not only to identify the approaching vehicle as a possible hazard but truly predict the worst. Remember the most dangerous places on two-way roads are the intersections.

3. Side impact collisions at traffic lights – I believe this collision can be avoided by constantly checking for oncoming and cross traffic while your traffic light is red. Don't wait until your light turns green to check for traffic. The article stated "red light running had increased more than three times the rate of all other types of fatal auto accidents." It seems that there are a lot more drivers who are "in a hurry" these days.
4. Collisions at unmarked (uncontrolled) intersections, in driveways and entries into shopping center parking lots – This one really surprised me because it would seem these would not be "high speed collisions." Remind your driver these are all different types of intersections and need to be handled cautiously.

As driver education instructor, Gary Magwood states, "Learn to use your eyes to look far down the road. Learn to spot problems before they happen. And remember the safest vehicles on the best designed highways on clear, sunny days are driven by fallible human beings who can crash into each other."

Just a Routine Trip to the Grocery Store?

About a year ago my wife and I were visiting our daughter and her family in Pensacola, Florida. It was early evening but not quite dark yet. I drove to the Winn Dixie to get a few grocery items. It was less than a ½ mile to the store. On my way back, everything seemed fine, but things changed quickly. I was driving a 2-way marked highway with a speed limit of 45 mph and I was approaching the side road where I needed to turn left. I properly signaled left, began gently braking for the turn, and identified I had no oncoming traffic.

What else do you think I needed to do to make sure this would be a SAFE left turn? Without thinking, I checked my rearview and had a vehicle behind me but this looked fine because I felt the car behind me was also slowing down. But when I checked my left sideview mirror, I was shocked! I was just about to make this "safe" left turn when unexpectedly I was being passed by a pickup truck that was 2 vehicles behind me. Oh my gosh!!! If I would have started into my left turn without checking my sideview mirror this truck could have struck the driver's side of my SUV! Remember this was a 45 mph zone and this vehicle was passing. This is a perfect example of why it is "illegal" to pass at or near an intersection. On just a routine trip to the grocery store, I could have been seriously injured or killed. Our rule in the driver ed car was every time you need to slow down, especially to turn or stop, check your mirrors, check your mirrors, check your mirrors! It is really ironic to consider that at this intersection, I could have been another "Good Driver that got killed!"

Author's Bio

Tom Hund taught Driver Education at Wesclin High School for twenty-one years. He also taught Business Law, coached boys' and girls' basketball and golf, and was the high school athletic director for twelve years. Prior to teaching at Wesclin, he taught and coached at St. Libory Grade School in St. Libory, Illinois for seven years. He lives with his wife Shelley in New Baden, Illinois. They have two children and two grandchildren.

Made in the USA
Monee, IL
18 February 2023

27507564R00090